Poets of Today

Poets of Today

A NEW AMERICAN ANTHOLOGY

edited by

WALTER LOWENFELS

with a prologue poem by

LANGSTON HUGHES

INTERNATIONAL PUBLISHERS   New York

COPYRIGHT ACKNOWLEDGMENTS

Second Printing, 1966

© copyright, 1964, BY WALTER LOWENFELS

Member Authors League of America

Library of Congress Catalog Card Number: 64–8443

Manufactured in the United States of America

Editor's Foreword

Tu Fu said a good poem lasts a thousand years. Will the poems in this book make it? I'm sure our epoch will be remembered, if not for poems, for things like Carbon 14 and Strontium 90. The 50's and 60's[1] are engraved on the earth in nuclear hieroglyphics. I'm not talking about the subject matter of this book, but the essential nuclear framework out of which the poems arise. No matter what our poets write about they cannot help reflect how it felt to be alive, in verse, since Hiroshima. In 1945 we put our hands into the mechanism of the universe and none of us have ever been the same. All relations are affected, human and inhuman, including relations between words in poems. When I see masks made by "primitive" Eskimos, Amerindians, Africans, I see mirror images of some of our poems that used the magic of the word to exorcise the evil, the terror that surrounds us, and to tune in on the vast potential of our age.

It was during the period when I was working on *Walt Whitman's Civil War*[2] that *Poets of Today* began to take shape. I found that we were known in many countries not only as the land of Whitman but also as the land of many other poets—living poets. This became even more apparent on a trip abroad when I had a chance to check on the state of poetry from Paris to Armenia.

From the Seine to the shadow of Mount Ararat, I was plied with questions about poets of the "beat generation," but nobody asked

1. Poets who began publishing after the war make up the bulk of the book. I include a half dozen of an older generation (including myself) all of whom had rebirths in the 50's and 60's and began to be read then by a new generation. I have noted elsewhere: "the poem doesn't consist just of words on a page. When the poem becomes a relationship between words and readers it really has been born."
2. New York, Alfred Knopf, 1961.

me about Ray Durem, Leslie Hedley, Don Gordon, Olga Cabral—
and dozens of others you will find in these pages.

At a café near the Sorbonne, Roger Asselineau[3] and I talked less
about Whitman than about three new French anthologies of
American poets. "But they do not show our real avant-garde," I
said. "Well, then, Monsieur Lowenfels, send us your choice."

In a snowbound village in Czechoslovakia last winter, while I was
being warmed with the proper spirits in a farmers' collective, the
stock-feeder asked me whether there were any young Negroes
among the best poets. In Warsaw, a young critic, who was doing a
doctoral thesis on Henry Miller, asked if I would send him poems
by Miller's successors. In Leningrad, as we waded through the slush
around the Fortress of Peter and Paul, the young and beautiful
guide who had been answering all our questions suddenly turned to
me and asked earnestly: "Mr. Lowenfels, what do you think of Jack
Kerouac?"

I returned home determined to uphold the honor of our country
with an anthology that would include other poets. I am convinced
that in this book they will show we have been producing a wide
range of poems—some of them relatively unknown, and yet as
contemporary and distinctly our own as jazz.

In these pages the reader will find poets as diverse as John
Beecher and Charles Bukowski, or Allen Ginsberg and Dalton
Trumbo. Ginsberg's poems are characterized by great rage and "a
love he celebrates without looking aside." And yet I don't find in
his Inferno that love of the future that makes Dante's hell bearable.
For Trumbo, on the other hand, "our children rise from the earth
like flowers lifting their faces for tomorrow's sun."

Dalton, you who saw the future even as you wrote your poetry
behind bars, and Allen, son of Jeremiah and Cassandra—what are
you doing in the same book? I could ask many other poets in this
collection similar questions.

And what about the book's exclusions? Why Ray Smith and not
William Snodgrass? Why Mari Evans and not May Swenson? Anyone who cares to pursue such questions further might do worse
than visit our national poetry archives in Washington. After a re-

3. Asselineau's *The Evolution of Walt Whitman* was published in English by
the Harvard University Press, 1962.

6

cording session in the Library of Congress the other day, I leafed through the catalog of poets whose recordings for the collection guarantee they will be heard as long as the library lasts—if somebody flips the right switch. I can testify that many poets missing from this anthology can be found in that vast collection of tapes.

My choice could not help being influenced by the kind of readers I anticipate: not only professionals in the art of reading poems, but the "divine average"—that new audience of millions that Whitman is still trying to reach. It is in this sense (envisioning and thus helping to create, a new class of readers) that I understand Shelley's salute to poets as the "unacknowledged legislators of the world."

Note that Shelley said "poets"—not "anthologies." A good poem outlasts any anthology. Whitman couldn't make the grade for Emerson's anthology, even though Emerson was one of the first to recognize his genius. This does not justify me in omitting poets I should have included. The 85 I do have (many of them for the first time in any anthology) show there is an avant-garde poetry in this country that is being ignored in most studies of American literature.

Each poet is represented by one poem. That doesn't mean that I consider Lucy Smith, for example, who writes short poems, less significant than Thomas McGrath, who has written longer ones.[4] My selections relate not only to the excellence of the specific poems but also to the way each fits into the book as a whole. I wanted the reader to have a collection that adds up to one over-all impact.

If, as Whitman said, "The United States themselves are the greatest poem," then the anthology can be considered one long poem by different poets, the subject of which is how it feels to be verbally alive in poems, in our country in our time. . . . Even if you are Afro-American. While there are now in print two recent anthologies of Negro poets, most general anthologies of American poetry exclude Negroes. In a review of what I called 15 years ago "The Oxford Book of (White) American Verse," I drew attention

4. The biographical notes at the end of the book will enable the reader to find additional work by each of the poets and discover for himself what riches each has to offer.

to segregation in poetry. Research in this field shows no improvement since then.[5]

Apparently other editors do not consider the kind of poems by the 20 Negroes I have included to be poetry.

My choice has been determined not by color but by what I respond to when "I hear the voice of America singing. . . ."

In a university library recently, I glanced over the reading list for a seminar in modern poetry. With one or two exceptions, none of the names in my anthology are listed. But Whitman, who had a hard time making the reading lists a century ago, is now there with a bang, or rather, a "yawp." I could hear his comment:

I was looking a long while for Intentions/ For a clue to the history of the past, and for these chants—and now I have found it,/ It is not in these paged fables in the libraries, (those I neither accept nor reject). It is no more in the legends than in all else. It is in the present—it is this earth today. . . . And in libraries I lie as one dumb, a gawk, or unborn, or dead. . . ."

As for the university poets omitted in my book, although certain critics say they represent our epoch, Truman Nelson wrote recently, "They have made a kind of authoritarian realm in which literature has fallen under control of academicians. Operating from the privileged sanctuaries of professorial chairs, they have focused on literary revivals rather than creativity."

What's the problem, then, in being creative and prophetic, rather than professorial and academic?

The minimum demands of creation: That something be given up, some of life be sacrificed, something done away with, so that something new arrives. There is an underground movement that keeps alive the creative biography of the earth. It is always changing, always new, giving us the latest word that everybody else misses. When the fire breaks out in the poet it melts words into a new mold. Then the poem of the world begins to flow from him.

Mays Landing, New Jersey —WALTER LOWENFELS
September 1964

5. One standard anthology still is restricted to the three Negro poets it has included since the 1930 Renaissance. In one other recent anthology, one new Negro poet appears. Otherwise there isn't even token representation.

8

EDITOR'S ACKNOWLEDGMENTS

To the Rabinowitz Foundation, for the generous grant which helped to make this book possible.

To Nan Braymer, my collaborator in this, as in all my other work.

To Lillian, my wife, for her helpful judgment and her faith when this book was only a project.

To my friends: the late Charles Humboldt, who made his vast experience and critical judgment available; Tom McGrath, for his patience and help, particularly in collecting some of the Pacific Coast poets; Leslie Woolf Hedley, for many valuable suggestions; François Hugot, for his special help in some of the research; and to my editor, James S. Allen, for his help in the final stages.

And to two without whom there would be no book; Marion Klugman, who typed at the beginning, and Judy Irrera, who typed at the end.

CONTENTS

11

12

13

Prologue

LANGSTON HUGHES

Let America Be America Again

Let America be America again.
Let it be the dream it used to be.
Let it be the pioneer on the plain
Seeking a home where he himself is free.

(America never was America to me.)

Let America be the dream the dreamers dreamed—
Let it be that great strong land of love
Where never kings connive nor tyrants scheme
That any man be crushed by one above.

(It never was America to me.)

O, let my land be a land where Liberty
Is crowned with no false patriotic wreath,
But opportunity is real, and life is free,
Equality is in the air we breathe.

(There's never been equality for me,
Nor freedom in this "homeland of the free.")

Say who are you that mumbles in the dark?
And who are you that draws your veil across the stars?

I am the poor white, fooled and pushed apart,
I am the red man driven from the land.

15

I am the refugee clutching the hope I seek—
But finding only the same old stupid plan
Of dog eat dog, of mighty crush the weak.
I am the Negro, "problem" to you all.
I am the people, humble, hungry, mean—
Hungry yet today despite the dream.
Beaten yet today—O, Pioneers!
I am the man who never got ahead,
The poorest worker bartered through the years.

Yet I'm the one who dreamt our basic dream
In that Old World while still a serf of kings,
Who dreamt a dream so strong, so brave, so true,
That even yet its mighty daring sings
In every brick and stone, in every furrow turned
That's made America the land it has become.
O, I'm the man who sailed those early seas
In search of what I meant to be my home—
For I'm the one who left dark Ireland's shore,
And Poland's plain, and England's grassy lea,
And torn from Black Africa's strand I came
To build a "homeland of the free."

The free?
Who said the free? Not me?
Surely not me? The millions on relief today?
The millions who have nothing for our pay
For all the dreams we've dreamed
And all the songs we've sung
And all the hopes we've held
And all the flags we've hung,
The millions who have nothing for our pay—
Except the dream we keep alive today.

O, let America be America again—
The land that never has been yet—
And yet must be—the land where every man is free.
The land that's mine—the poor man's, Indian's, Negro's, ME—

16

Who made America,
Whose sweat and blood, whose faith and pain,
Whose hand at the foundry, whose plow in the rain,
Must bring back our mighty dream again.

O, yes,
I say it plain,
America never was America to me,
And yet I swear this oath—
America will be!

GEORGE ABBE

From *Changed*

I saw a man turned into money:
His head became a bank vault door
in which the wheels were seen to hurry,
the valves were heard to quaintly purr.

The breast was soft as brown purse leather
in which the bones were solid coin.
The bullion heart, held fast forever,
fed stocks and bonds through copper veins. . .

And looking down, I saw, amazed
that the reproductive organs set
in wax and most conspicuously placed,
were nothing more than cancelled checks.

GEORGE HUSTON BASS

Life Cycle in the Delta

First Daddy
Then Mama
Then Me

First Plant
Then Chop
Then Pick

19

PLANT!
CHOP!
PICK!

daddy
mama
me.

JOHN BEECHER

A Veteran's Day of Recollection

We'd liberated Naples and the Wops
had come aboard to work cargo. This hungry
Spik slipped a can of rations underneath
his filthy rags. We drilled him. At Marseilles
we mowed a stevedore down for pilfering
some Spam. The Battle of the Bulge was on,
V-bombs had knocked out Antwerp but the God
damned Frogs struck every ship of ours in port.
P-40's shot up Palermo for the hell
of it. Pinpoint objectives? Tenements!
Krauts wrecked Le Havre's docks and blew. The town
was open. Flying Fortresses blasted
it flat and left some thirty thousand dead
allies of ours. Brother, those ruins stank!
GI's in Germany went "one to shoot
and three to loot." We always gave
a Hershey to the frauleins that we ganged.

ART BERGER

Bedford Avenue

At the ghetto end
of the Bedford stem
black children space out

on the furnace
called the street

Yet down a piece
on the very same drag
the air sings with the kiss
of cool salt water;
red roses and green lawns
draped in mists of spray.

A whole world's pain
spilled from flats
to pavements ablaze
at morning
and the vulture
stalks by noon.

ALVAH BESSIE

For My Dead Brother

(*Aaron Lopoff, 1938*)

The moon was full that night in Aragon . . .
we sat in the black velvet shadow
of the hazel (called *avellano* there);
the men lay sleeping, sprawled on the packed earth
in their blankets (like the dead) . . .

With dawn we'd move in double files
down to the Ebro, cross in boats,
and many lying there relaxed
would lie relaxed across the river
(but without their blankets).

He said: "You started something, baby—"
(I was thirty-four; he ten years less;
he was my captain; I his adjutant)

21

"—you started something, baby," Aaron said,
"when you came to Spain."

Across the yellow river
there was a night loud with machine guns
and the harmless popcorn crackle
of hand grenades bursting pink and green,
and he was gone and somehow Sam found me in the dark,
bringing Aaron's pistol, wet with blood.
He said:
    "The last thing Aaron said
    was, 'Did we take the hill?'
    I told him, 'Sure.' "
Aaron, we did not take the hill.
We lost in Spain. Aaron,
I know, finally, what you meant that night
under the black shadow of the *avellano*,
sitting here in prison twelve years later.
We did not take the hill, *mi commandante*,
but o! the plains that we have taken
and the mountains, rivers, cities,
deserts, flowing valleys, seas!
You may sleep . . . sleep, my brother, sleep.

MILLEN BRAND

Local Light

Lightning is local.
First from its pool of cloud
coiled like a serpent,
it flicks its tongue here and there
toward the ground.
First that round
of coiled cloud over a neighborhood,
and then one or a few

22

hot fangs following the tongue.
At Pat Giagnocavo's, up the lane,
is a tree notched with the heat
that passed its heart and burned
out along a chain to a goat
and notched her heart too.
At Pennsburg,
two baseball players shared
a single blazing strike. Summer flies
north and in Vermont the writhing folds
bite down a tree
in a small cemetery where
thunder dies into the grass.
In Minnesota, a lake of darkening sky
floats over a reflecting lake
and lets down a shine of yellow hair
toward the Mississippi, the father.
Now the clouds coil in the air
high above Sangre de Cristo
in New Mexico, above Chimayo,
glowing red in the evening
with the blood of Christ. The Jemez Canyon
in shadow catches the flashes
against the cliffs. At this altitude,
eight thousand feet, the fang of heat
touches the moisture in a tree,
turning it to steam, and simply
blows the tree up.
A fire may start in the duff
of long-needled ponderosa pine,
smouldering two days, damped down by the rain,
then break out its living flag.
In California, the infrequent storms
signal like canopies shaken
and gleaming along the seams of noon.
A hiss of light covers the jacaranda
and stops where the banana tree wavers
in its earthen socket. Uphill,

23

the decomposed granite brightens,
mimicking gold, and rolls with the boats
of live oak leaves. In Pennsylvania,
fire is immediate.
Two miles from Pat Giagnocavo's tree,
the snake's bite startled a barn
and the flames roared into the rain,
eating all the wood, leaving
perfectly vertical stone walls
as clean as ideas of walls.
Hard to think, in sunlight,
that pools of fire and death
wait in the sky, an igneous dream
man makes deliberate
with his own fangs.

GEORGE BRATT

AWOL

Where are you Carl Schulte, former sharper man for H. Quandt &
    Son?
Did you finally call the turn on wishful thinking
and really go back to Chicago?
And was your rendezvous with Carl Schulte, furniture worker
of two decades ago, a success?
Or did you simply fail to snap out of your vacation pay check
    drunk?

You didn't leave us, your shopmates, much of a forwarding address.
Just "Not here" via your old Valencia St. hotel,
and a blank space in our local business agent's report.
Now you are an unsettled memory that stands punctually by
each morning ready to start up the machines.

Although you were witty, loved musical shows and had a
voice to appeal to receptive women,

noon-hour sessions with you were no great cultural treat.
It took job action to get you to vote at the polls,
and the threat of a five-dollar fine to integrate you
with a union meeting.

But that long silent partnership we had with you!
Those grinding, interminable, laborious hours when Schulte,
pencil in hat, was king,
the dust and crap spurting off the shrieking shaper
and haloing you truly as an adorable human being!—
Where now are we to find the clue to him?—
In the unsigned door jambs of sundry homes?
Hidden away in the machined drawers of their kitchen cabinets?

In the thousand nameless places where workers have left
the token of their sweat, sacrifice and devotion?

Where are you now, Brother Schulte?
Where are you, fellow-worker?

MARION BUCHMAN

First-Born

I saw no infant
but rather, the frightened never-understood
young girl
the matron who hated old age
and then the old woman
embroidering life with memory's heavy thread
I heard no child cry
but storms rage
I saw time erode even the last inscription
on her stone
and so I wept
when they brought her in.

CHARLES BUKOWSKI

The Day I Kicked a Bankroll Out the Window

and, I said, you can take your rich aunts and uncles
and grandfathers and fathers
and all their lousy oil
and their seven lakes
and their wild turkey
and buffalo
and the whole state of Texas
meaning, your crow-blasts
and your Saturday night boardwalks,
and your 2-bit library
and your crooked councilmen
and your pansy artists—
you can take all these
and your weekly newspaper
and your famous tornadoes
and your filthy floods
and all your yowling cats
and your subscription to *Life*,
and shove them, baby,
shove them.
I can handle a pick and ax again (I think)
and I can pick up
25 bucks for a 4-rounder (maybe);
sure, I'm 38
but a little dye can pinch the gray
out of my hair;
and I can still write a poem (sometimes),
don't forget *that*, and even if
they don't pay off,
it's better than waiting for death and oil,
and shooting wild turkey,
and waiting for the world to begin.

26

all right, bum, she said,
get out.

what? I said.

get out. you've thrown your last tantrum.
I'm tired of your damned tantrums:
you're always acting like a
character
in an O'Neill play.

but I'm different, baby,
I can't help
it.

you're different, all right!
God, how different!
don't slam
the door
when you leave.

but, baby, I *love* your
money!

you never once said
you loved me!

what do you want
a liar or a
lover?

you're neither; out, bum,
out!

... but baby!

go back to O'Neill!

I went to the door,

27

softly closed it and walked away,
thinking: all they want
is a wooden Indian
to say yes and no
and stand over the fire and
not raise too much hell;
but you're getting to be
an old man, kiddo:
next time play it closer
to the
vest.

OLGA CABRAL

From *Empire State*

I am a prisoner of bones
of keyrings habits teeth and hair
I am a tenant of torn skies
I am a runner in the air
of escalators that ascend
a hundred storeys to a chair
    high
        where Old Fireye
            punches the astral timeclock.

And from this mountain of aluminum
I loose strange birds upon
the city, poems in guise
of pigeons, doves by teletype—
creatures of bolt and cam
spun by my typewriter
    keys,
        mechanical mysteries
            flying over the watertowers:

                    Toggle Switch
                        Kicker Baffle
                    Drive Shaft
And again it is
jobday another
morning in the gray
beginning when five million
alarm clocks salute the sun
in unison and the
Flow Indicator Top Connector
throws the Master Switch wherefore
on the Remote Control Panel
of the Photoelectric Scanner I'm
spotted
seized
swept sorted scanned
pinched punched processed pressed
dissolved digested
soulmashed
to join the oozing gray indifferent
lifesludge
of primal protozoan human logjam
that feeds
the great soul factory and
greases the great big wheels

And deep down dark under
bedrock riverbed and tungsten
bones in subcellars
in the very solar-plexus of it all
I'm chewed spat cannonaded through lightyears
and awful vaults of voids
where all the money of the world is kept
past timeclocks punching in and out like mad,
till suddenly I'm there—
sole occupant and heir,
        the slave
            of the chair
                in the air . . .

ALVARO CARDONA-HINE

Bulosan Now

had to be
she would come
with telegram
stop instead of comma
rest in peace

with cable
come in place of reason
rest on earth

had to be
your absent-minded flesh
would answer
in time and wiry body
and we would be companions
beyond a nasty seam

but no moment knows you dead Bulosan
or gone or vacant or destroyed
intervals are vaults
where death can bandy us
in a wild arch
but between its twin possessions
spring
the wasted eternal instants
of life
and the flicker and the crush
fermenting
in the clasp of generations
the permanence of those
who like you
gave yes an answer

oh persecuted of autumn
hunted by door and day

30

for instigating orchards
here is where abuse
kneels in your presence

accomplished now
fulfilled in lesser shadow
are loaves of bread
sturdy ladders
inches of protection
growth by womb of membership and dues
this done by daring lift
the rocks of the forehead
into clammy notebooks
stuffing margins upon jails
by abandoning your hungry fingers
to the mercy of suspect pages

peculiar feeling that
when freedom shares a fingerprint with fear
when a sick lung has to share its milk with ulcers
or when a country lane is blocked
and unionists dragged
immediately before the innumerable agonies
have lips
or your knuckles have bruised
the tender radiance of America

strange crammed feeling
by dint of hounds behind the life expectancy
of a moment
Philippino of I suppose
tight skin upon fine bones
you were brave
in those days
your manhood
of smashed testicles
standing by the brothered stranger
like a little flag frayed at the edges
of incapable bullets

brave
and I wonder
at how wide the interval
between the center of Carlos Bulosan
and the ifs and ohs of a careless funeral
that are gently setting the date for a reunion
I can raise the thankful inkwells of my voice
to place you squarely and concretely among this brutal
    instant of life
in irreplaceable fashion
as one who knew how to forever subsist later upon *now*

JOHN WILLIAM CORRINGTON

From *Communique: I*

1

Life at the peak of the Radiant Days
    is dream
broadcasting rigid tendrils through
    the sleepcaught,
fleshing the great poison,
    the continental cancer,
    the imperial ailment,
booming the uranium age.

And khaki declaration drums and
    teeters,
hurtles erect and bannerwide:

who plies the nightshift until
    fail safe,
who blesses the smoking fleet?

       * * *

       —corporal jesus
commander grinly

said—see that hill
the one with three sad trees
take it

    * * *

Yet soldier leavens the thundering grass,
and earth bent in rainy continuum
leaches downward great loamy tears
for all the dead warriors:
the melting gunmen,
old bones of poorshots scattered
in gin wars, land wars, pride wars, sin wars,
and (of course) the sterling campaigns,
and some most youngish foot yet mopes
paths of glory
where deep worms patrol new catacombs
guessing potential bone in
darkness the size of end . . .

4

Analyze the pathology of poisoned spirit
that feeds on a pension of hopeful
wrath.

Erect a minimal table to the armoured
impostures sealed and nourished in
a wilderness of hearts.

Render statistics of amputation, together
with filmed excerpts of surgeons gone
mad, of nurses coyly munching something
odd, of mothers aborting with pencils
fearing the face of their young, of
fathers dancing into geigermist with
the XXIX armycorpse.
Check
Check

33

                    Check
          It is finished.
                              except for that hill
          where the singing
                    will not stop
                    where the bones chill and
          wonderfully white
                              are strumming tomorrow
          awake
                    We gunned and gunned—
                    We bombed and bombed
                              till the sad trees
          bent into belcanto, till bullets turned and
          blossomed back to us, till pits healed them-
          selves and propellers whispered a treason of
          love and rest.

                    This is to inform the
          commander (who grims an ending grin)
                                        We have
          gone over to the flowers,
          defected to our fathers.   We will die in
                                                    pairs
          alive till then: no bone has lied
                    no tree has borne the truth
          in vain. At last the grass is springing
          syllables:
                    we are finished with thunder
                              (yes the commander grims)

                    It is finished. Even a hill can be plowed,
          and bones broken to wheat.

          Dream of an aria tilted to summer,
          an alphabet breathing plans: are you praying?

          Already. Now then

                              34

GREGORY CORSO

Uccello

They will never die on that battlefield
nor the shade of wolves   recruit their hoard like brides of
wheat on all horizons waiting there to consume battle's end
There will be no dead to tighten their loose bellies
no heap of starched horses to redsmash their bright eyes
    or advance their eat of dead
They would rather hungersulk with mad tongues
than believe that on that field no man dies

They will never die who fight so embraced
breath to breath   eye knowing eye   impossible to die
or move   no light seeping through   no maced arm
nothing but horse outpanting horse   shield brilliant upon
shield   all made starry by the dot ray of a helmeted eye
ah   how difficult to fall between those knitted lances
And those banners!   angry as to flush insignia across its
    erasure of sky
You'd think he'd paint his armies by the coldest rivers
have rows of iron skulls flashing in the dark
    You'd think it impossible for any man to die
each combatant's mouth is a castle of song
each iron fist a dreamy gong   flail resounding flail
        like cries of gold
how I dream to join such a battle!
a silver man on a black horse with red standard and striped
    lance   never to die but to be endless
        a golden prince of pictorial war

CARLOS CORTEZ

Outa Work Blues

Well it's a long time on the street
And the rockin' chair money's
    all gone,
It's a long, long time on the
    street
And the rockin' chair money's
    all gone.
    I'm down to rollin' my own
    And pickin' butts off the lawn.

Went to the employment office
To see what I could find,
I went to the employment office
To see what I could find
    Six hundred other people
        there
    Same thing on their mind.

Told the interviewer
I'd do anything but shovel crap,
I told the interviewer
I'd do anything but shovel crap,
    He told me he was sorry
There was only one opening
    for that.

When I was drawing
    compensation
They'd hang any job on my neck
Yes, when I was drawing
    compensation

They'd hang any job on my neck
But now that old rockin'
    chair's busted
They won't let me past
    the first desk.

President said on television
That things was mighty fine
The president said on television
That things was mighty fine

    Man at the supermarket
        tells me
    No groceries sold on time.

MARGARET DANNER

The Elevator Man Adheres to Form

I am reminded, by the tan man who wings
the elevator of Rococo art. His ways
are undulating waves that shepherd and swing
us cupid-like from floor to floor.

He sweethearts us
with polished pleasantries; gallantly
flourishing us up and up. No casual "Hi's" from him.

His greetings, Godspeedings, display his Ph. D.
aplomb, and I should feel like a cherubim,
be fleur-de-lis and pastel-shell-like, but

instead, I vision other tan and deeper much than tan
early-Baroque-like men, who (seeing themselves still strut-
lessly groping, winding down subterranean

grottoes of injustice, down dark spirals) feel
with such tortuous, smoked-stone greyed intensity
that they exhale a hurricane of gargoyles, then reel

into it. I see these others boggling in their misery
and wish this elevator artisan would fill his flourishing form
with warmth for them and turn his lettered zeal
toward lifting them above their crippling storm.

RICHARD DAVIDSON

Play the Last March Slowly

(An epitaph for Hyman Levine, friend, killed in the Korean
War.)

Someone put a bullet through his orphan brain
Somewhere in the smiling eastern evening
When air swam through pits of broken shells and
Tearing whistles saluted blood-drenched bandages.
Someone kissed him out of this life with a right hook
Of steel above the base of the forehead
Changing his wonderful, groping condition.
The muscles relaxed; long adventure in the secret night
Over.
Someone grabbed three dreams of twisted youth and shook
Them into nothing.
Someone blew the ripe, rich horn of the angel of death
And he laughed at its throat and winked in its face
But it took him along nevertheless.
Nevertheless they had a funeral.
Nevertheless four bands played glowingly out of tune.
Nevertheless fifty fellow orphans lined up in the rain
To take their hats off;
To kiss him goodbye across the bridge of night.
Nevertheless the polished senator with the bulging
Toupee spoke rapturously about sacrifice,

About glory,
About the wonderful horsemen who would come on
Strong white chargers and lead him home.
Nevertheless the grass grew brighter in the morning
Sun of dying twilight;
The birds who knew death intimately;
Who pipe organ music over stilted meadows wept in
Their beaks.
They remembered him for he pulled their tails and
Made them cry.
Someone put a bullet through his orphan brain
Somewhere in the smiling eastern evening.

WALT DELEGALL

From *Elegy for a Lady*

(Billy Holiday,
—Lady—Day—,
famous Blues Singer,
died under tragic
circumstances, a
drug-addict) . . .

A lady's dead and a
Gentleman killed her. A
Gentleman named morality or
Maybe life. I'm not exactly
Sure, but he killed her. He
Killed her in South Philly back
In '47 at the Attucks Hotel. He
Killed her in Baltimore in 1928.
He snuffed out her life with
New York cabaret licenses. He
Murdered her with judges and
Federal Women's Penitentiaries. He

Battered her with Afro
Headlines in 48 point gothic
Type. He strangled her with
Slander and pointed fingers. He
Killed her and dragged her by
Her heels from the end of his
Chariot. And her only anodyne
Was the naked blues and her
Only relief was to use and use,
Percy baby, she paid her dues. . . .

RAY DUREM

Award

[A Gold Watch to the FBI Man (who has followed me) for 25
Years.]

Well, old spy
looks like I
led you down some pretty blind alleys,
took you on several trips to Mexico,
fishing in the high Sierras,
jazz at the Philharmonic.
You've watched me all your life,
I've clothed your wife,
put your two sons through college.
what good has it done?
sun keeps rising every morning.
Ever see me buy an Assistant President?
or close a school?
or lend money to Somoza?
I bought some after-hours whiskey in L.A.
but the Chief got his pay.
I ain't killed no Koreans,
or fourteen-year-old boys in Mississippi

40

neither did I bomb Guatemala,
or lend guns to shoot Algerians.
I admit I took a Negro child
to a white rest room in Texas,
but she was my daughter, only three,
and she had to pee,
and I just didn't know what to do,
would you?
see, I'm so light, it don't seem right
to go to the colored rest room;
my daughter's brown, and folks frown on that in Texas,
I just don't know how to go to the bathroom in the free world!

Now, old FBI man,
you've done the best you can,
you lost me a few jobs,
scared a couple landlords,
You got me struggling for that bread,
but I ain't dead.
and before its all through,
I may be following you!

BOB DYLAN

Hard Rain's A-Gonna Fall

Where have you been my blue eyed
    son?
Where have you been my darlin'
    young one?
I've stumbled on the side of twelve
    misty mountains
I've walked and I've crawled on six
    crooked highways
I've stepped in the middle of seven
    sad forests

41

I've been out in front of a dozen
        dead oceans
I've been ten thousand miles in the mouth
        of a graveyard
And it's a hard, hard, hard, hard,
And it's a hard rain's a gonna fall.

    What have you seen my blue eyed
        son?
    What have you seen my darlin'
        young one?
I saw a new born babe with wild wolves
        all around it;
I saw a highway of golden with nobody
        on it;
I saw a black branch with blood that
        kept dripping;
I saw a room full of men with their
        hammers a-bleeding;
I saw a white ladder all covered with
        water;
I saw ten thousand talkers whose tongues
        were all broken;
I saw guns and sharp swords in the
        hands of young children.
And it's a hard, hard, hard, hard,
And it's a hard rain's a gonna fall.

    What did you hear my blue eyed
        son?
    What did you hear my darlin'
        young one?
I heard the sound of a thunder that
        roared out a warning;
I heard the roar of a wave that could
        drown the whole world;
I heard one hundred drummers whose
        hands were a-blazing;

42

I heard ten thousand whispering and
        nobody listening;
I heard one person starve, I heard
        many persons laughing;
I heard the song of a poet who died in
        the gutter,
I heard the sounds of a clown who cried
        in the alley;
I heard the sound of one person who
        cried he was human.
And it's a hard, hard, hard, hard,
And it's a hard rain's a gonna fall.

    Who did you meet my blue eyed
        son?
    Who did you meet my darlin'
        young one?
I met a young child beside a dead pony;
I met a white man who walked a black
        dog;
I met a young woman whose body was
        burning;
I met a young girl, she gave me a
        rainbow;
I met one man who was wounded in love;
I met another man who was wounded in
        hatred.
And it's a hard, hard, hard, hard,
And it's a hard rain's a gonna fall.

    What'll you do now my blue eyed
        son?
    What'll you do now my darlin'
        young one?
I'm a-going back out fore the rain
        starts a falling;
I'll walk to the depths of the deepest
        dark forest;

Where the people are many and their
    hands are all empty;
Where the pellets of poison are flooding
    their waters;
Where the home in the valley meets the
    damp dirty prison;
Where the executioner's face is always
    well hidden;
Where the hunger is ugly, where souls
    are forgotten;
Where black is the color, where none is
    the number;
And I'll tell it and speak it and think it
    and breathe it;
And reflect from the mountain so all
    souls can see it;
Then I'll stand on the ocean until I
    start sinking;
But I'll know my song well before I
    start singing.
And it's hard, hard, hard, hard,
And it's hard rain's a gonna fall.

EILEEN EGAN

Hibakusha

She looked up
to see the whole sky explode
into shattering orange.
The color of goldfish, she said it was.

She was not yet three.
In May she had watched the great paper fish
golden and red
fill the sky space above her.

44

The karp-kites flew for the hopes
of millions of Japanese boys.
The wonder of the billowing things
held her black eyes all day long.

When she looked up that August morning
the sky was a world of moving light,
goldfish light,
that sucked into her head in two burning shafts.

When they examined her body for hurt,
they lifted the eyelids
to discover melted eyeballs.

Not only as memory
does the color persist for her.
A terrible tiredness sometimes possesses her
and the bright orange returns and fills her skull to bursting.

Seasons go by unseen
except by her fingers.
She marks spring, summer, autumn
in making mock flowers,
knowing in her hands the forms
of spring blossoms, summer roses, autumn chrysanthemums.
And often she folds paper cranes
for health and long life,
and now as prayers for peace.

'It is May again and I am blind.'
was the sign a man carried in a city of Europe,
and for joy—and guilt—of being sighted,
men, women and children filled his begging bowl.

'It is August and I am eyeless,'
she could say to us.
But she is silent and asks for no alms.
By the work of her hands she earns her daily rice.

For guilt of her what shall we do—
we in whose name the bowl of the sky was filled
with death the color of goldfish,
death that billowed into a mighty flower of evil—
for guilt of the melted eyeballs of Hiroshima.

MARI EVANS

Status Symbol

i
Have Arrived

i
am the
New Negro

i
am the result of
President Lincoln
World War I
and Paris
the
Red Ball Express
white drinking fountains
sitdowns and
sit-ins
Federal Troops
Marches on Washington
        and
prayer meetings . . .

today
They hired me
it
is a status

                              job . . .
                              along
                              with my papers
                              They
                              gave me my
                              Status Symbol
                              the
                              key
                              to the
                              White . . . Locked . . .
                              John

LAWRENCE FERLINGHETTI

Tentative Description of a Dinner Given to Promote
the Impeachment of President Eisenhower

After it became obvious that the strange rain would never stop
And after it became obvious that the President was doing every-
    thing in his power
And after it became obvious that the President's general staff was
    still in contact with the President deep in the heart of Georgia
    while deep in the heart of South America the President's
    left-hand man was proving all the world loves an American
And after it became obvious that the strange rain would never
    stop and that Old Soldiers never drown and that roses in the
    rain had forgotten the word for bloom and that perverted
    pollen blown on sunless seas was eaten by irradiated fish who
    spawned up cloudleaf streams and fell onto our dinnerplates
And after it became obvious that the President was doing every-
    thing in his power to make the world safe for nationalism his
    brilliant military mind never having realized that nationalism
    itself was the idiotic superstition which would blow up the
    world
And after it became obvious that the President nevertheless still
    carried no matter where he went in the strange rain the little
    telegraph key which like a can opener could be used instantly

47

to open but not to close the hot box of final war if not to
waylay any stray asinine action by any stray asinine second
lieutenant pressing any strange button anywhere far away over
an arctic ocean thus illuminating the world once and for all
And after it became obvious that the law of gravity was still in
effect and that what blows up must come down on everyone
including white citizens
And after it became obvious that the Voice of America was really
the Deaf Ear of America and that the President was unable
to hear the underprivileged natives of the world shouting
No Contamination Without Representation in the strange
rain from which there was no escape—except Peace
And after it became obvious that the word Truth had only a
comic significance to the Atomic Energy Commission while
the President danced madly to mad Admiral Straus waltzes
wearing special atomic earplugs which prevented him from
hearing Albert Schweitzer and nine thousand two hundred
and thirty-five other scientists telling him about spastic generations and blind boneless babies in the rain from which there
was no escape—except Peace
And after it became obvious that the President was doing everything in his power to get thru the next four years without
eating any of the crates of irradiated vegetables wellwishers
had sent him from all over and which were filling the corridors
and antechamber and bedchambers and chamberpots in the
not-so-white House not to mention all the other various Golf
Houses scattered thruout the land of prosperity
And after it became obvious that the Great Soldier had become
the Great Conciliator who had become the Great Com-
promiser who had become the Great Fence Sitter who actually had heard of the Supreme Court's decision to desegregate
the land of the free and had not only heard of it but had
actually read it
And after it became obvious that the President had gone to Gettys-
burg fourscore and seven years ago and had given his Gettys-
burg Address to the postman and so dedicated himself to the
unfinished task

Then it was that the natives of the Republic began assembling in the driving rain from which there was no escape—except Peace

And then it was that no invitations had to be sent out for the great testimonial dinner except to politicians whose respected names would lend weight to the product but who did not come anyway suspecting the whole thing was a plot to save the world from the clean bomb from which there was no escape—except Peace

And women who still needed despair to look truly tragic came looking very beautiful and very tragic indeed since there was despair to spare

And some men also despaired and sat down in Bohemia and were too busy to come

But other men came whose only political action during the past twenty years had been to flush a protesting toilet and run

And babies came in their carriages carrying irradiated dolls and holding onto crazy strings of illuminated weather ballons filled with Nagasaki air

And those who had not left their TV sets long enough to notice the weather in seven years now came swimming thru the rain holding their testimonials

And those came who had never marched in sports car protest parades and those came who had never been arrested for sailing a protesting Golden Rule in unpacific oceans

And Noah came in his own Ark looking surprisingly like an outraged Jesus Christ and cruised about flying his pinion and picking up two of each beast that wanted to be preserved in the rain which was raining real cats and dogs and from which there was no escape—except Peace

And those came who had not been kidnapped on the streets of San Francisco by a special patriotic gestapo designed to make America safe for democracy

And peddlers came in lead jockstraps selling hotdogs and rubber American flags and waving petitions proclaiming it Unamerican to play golf on the same holy days that clean bombs were set off on time

And finally after everyone who was anyone and after everyone who was no one had arrived and after every soul was seated and waiting for the symbolic mushroom soup to be served and for the keynote speeches to begin

The President himself came in
Took one look around and said
We Resign

VINCENT FERRINI

From *Mirandum*

THE SEA

The sea is up
to the eyebrows

galloping over dragon heads
churning the pebbles in

the wind a promise
present and far away

under water lightning is
handcuffed to lightning

a black fire-breathing
stallion

champing for halcyon meadows
tethered under sea

EDWARD FIELD

From *Ode to Fidel Castro*

I

O Boy-God, Muse of Poets
Come sit on my shoulders while I write
Cuddle up and fill my poem with love
And even while I fly on billows of inspiration
Don't forget to tickle me now and then
For I am going to write on World Issues
which demands laughter where we most believe . . .

My subject, Dear Muse, is Fidel Castro
Rebellissimo and darling of the Spanish-American lower classes
A general who adopted for his uniform
The work clothes of the buck private and the beard of the saints
A man fit for ruling a great nation
But who only has an island.

Irene, the beautiful Cuban, has his picture over her bed
Between Rudolph Valentino and the Blessed Virgin—
He stands large and flabby between the perfect body and the purest
    soul
And one dove for crown standing on his head—
He is not afraid of birdshit, his face is radiant.

The Hotel Teresa in Harlem is a dumpy landmark in a slum
But when Fidel Castro went there to stay
And when Nikita Khrushchev went up and hugged and kissed
    him for being Mr. Wonderful
Right out in public (they get away with it those foreigners)
Then Harlem became the capitol of the world
And the true home of the United Nations . . .

BOMBS GOING OFF ALL OVER HAVANA

In Rockefeller Center the Cuban Tourist Office is closed
And across the skating rink men are putting up

51

The world's largest Christmas tree which will never be Christian
Even if you cut it down, make it stand on cement, decorate it
  with balls
It will still scream for the forest, like a wild animal
Like the gods who love freedom and topple to the saws of com-
  merce
The gods who frighten us half to death in our dreams with their
  doings
And disappear when we need them most, awake.

By the time you see this, Fidel, you might not even exist anymore
My government is merciless and even now
The machine to destroy you is moving into action. . . .

But I wish you well Fidel Castro
And if you do succeed in making that island
The tropic paradise God meant it to be
I'll be the first to cheer and come for a free visit if invited.

So you're not perfect, poets don't look for perfect
It's your spirit we love and the glamour of your style
I hope someday the cameras of the world
Are turned on you and me in some spot like Harlem
And then you'll get a kiss that will make Khrushchev's be for-
  gotten
A kiss of the poet, that will make you truly good
The way you meant to be.

GENE FRUMKIN

In the Margin of the Text

Myself standing in the margin of the text
which is Cuba:
black soldiers on pages of sugar;
standing beside a sycamore

52

in a saucer of flowers,
royal palms overlooking
the rooftops like giraffes,
the morning cruising around me
on a slow bicycle.
I glance at the jagged edges of heaven to the north
and know that elsewhere men move ahead
the hands of the sun.

                        But in our city
Cuba is not a place but a checkerboard,
Castro is a cartoon
and his government, a crime.
I think I'm living in a secondhand world
in which too often I've surprised myself kneeling
or reaching for the sky.

                       The poems I wanted to write
for those Batista murdered in their honest passion,
for the saplings of the revolution,
for Castro's beard and other prophecies
are out of sight, political prisoners somewhere.

Instead, I watch the snails
on the walkway,
listen to the children
in the house,
to the conscience of the bluejay
on the limb,
and feel immortal as a housefly.

DAVID GALLATIN

Put Your Key

Put your key in the lock of violence
Turn it
Suns drop from sky
Oceans heave up their drowned skulls
No it is only you
Looking in your mirror

There he is
Running through three fields at once
Grasping after shifts of shadow forms and winds
His skin in flames everywhere he runs
To find the true rain the true water the true rain
No it is only you
Reading a book in bed

Tomorrow morning
Shadows floating in his throat

Start to tear at
These triple puzzle walls
Filled with hidden mirrors
Bats burst out at noon
Hungers stagger off to dream with drunks asleep in urinals
Put your key in the lock of violence
Turn it
Mental oceans weave new chains
Liberty in shadows
Death's black monks dancing on all the roofs
A star moves down the street
No it is only you
Walking your way to work for money

ESTELLE GERSHGOREN

We Are Gathered Together

the bread
    popping out of hot ovens
lobsters walking on the sand
    dripping wet life

Inland they are paving the roads
    with husks of corn
Waiting inside a daisy
    for the leaves to be plucked
    for the something to happen
For the coral of the sea
    to be counted
For the census of lost minds
    to be taken.

They are gathered here today
For that reason
To count the choked throats
The rustling of skirts
    blowing away in salt air.

They are gathered together
Dearly beloved of beggars
Sandwiched ears of corn
Threshed by their real souls
Into pieces of white sand.

They bought a ticket
    to the third star
Beyond
    the horizons of children
The islands of the cyclic migration
    of tourists.

55

Beyond that they are gathered
    to praise no name
    to sing no songs
    to ask one question.
To the smoke of bonfires
    gathered in the arms of children.

Why are the judges of land
    the earthquakes?
Why between day and day
    there is no food?
Between song and eulogy
    there is no truth?
Why are the governors
    wearing out
        the thin feet
            of our children?

We are leaving the fields
    to your planting
The fires
    to your black stubble
Our songs
    to the beggars
Who carry away the winter
    under their coats.
Our memories
    to your white beards
Our sinking dreams
    hanging on the highest branches.
Somehow
    we will get on
After
    the sunrise
Before
    dark
We will eat
    new food

Sing
    new songs
Write down
    the dreams
        of our weddings
And the candles
    on Friday evenings
Our prayers
    for the dead only
And our dances
    for the new born.

Somewhere
    in the darkness
        where we stumble
We will find at the edge of our labor
A road map
    asking for travellers.

We have gathered together
Because the loneliness
    is unbearable
Alone
    we can do nothing.
Together
    we carry distant voices
On the shoulders of children
        unborn.

JACK GILBERT

The Abnormal Is Not Courage

The Poles rode out from Warsaw against the German
Tanks on horses. Rode knowing, in sunlight, with sabers.
A magnitude of beauty that allows me no peace.
And yet this poem would lessen that day. Question

The bravery. Say it's not courage. Call it a passion.
Would say courage isn't that. Not at its best.
It was impossible, and with form. They rode in sunlight.
Were mangled. But I say courage is not the abnormal.
Not the marvelous act. Not Macbeth with fine speeches.
The worthless can manage in public, or for the moment.
It is too near the whore's heart: the bounty of impulse,
And the failure to sustain even small kindness.
Not the marvelous act, but the evident conclusion of being.
Not strangeness, but a leap forward of the same quality.
Accomplishment. The even loyalty. But fresh.
Not the Prodigal Son, nor Faustus. But Penelope.
The thing steady and clear. Then the crescendo.
The real form. The culmination. And the exceeding.
Not the surprise. The amazed understanding. The marriage,
Not the month's rapture. Not the exception. The beauty
That is of many days. Steady and clear.
It is the normal excellence, of long accomplishment.

ALLEN GINSBERG

From *Kaddish*

(*For Naomi Ginsberg, 1894–1956*)

. . . O Russian faced, woman on the grass, your long black
hair is crowned with flowers, the mandolin is on your knees—
    Communist beauty, sit here married in the summer among
daisies, promised happiness at hand—
    holy mother, now you smile on your love, your world
is born anew, children run naked in the field spotted with
dandelions,
    they eat in the plum tree grove at the end of the meadow
and find a cabin where a white-haired Negro teaches the mystery
of his rainbarrel—
    blessed daughter come to America, I long to hear your

voice again, remembering your mother's music, in the Song of
the Natural Front—

O glorious muse that bore me from the womb, gave suck
first mystic life & taught me talk and music, from whose pained
head I first took Vision—

Tortured and beaten in the skull—What mad hallucinations
of the damned that drive me out of my own skull to seek
Eternity till I find Peace for Thee, O Poetry—and for all
humankind call on the Origin.

Death which is the mother of the universe!—Now wear
your nakedness forever, white flowers in your hair, your marriage
sealed behind the sky—no revolution might destroy that
maidenhood—

O beautiful Garbo of my Karma . . .

DON GORDON

The Kimono

Celebrate the season of the death
    of the city.
Celebrate the women in the newsreel,
    the print of her kimono
Burned in her back. Celebrate the bamboo
    leaves, the folded fans.

Exhibit A, formerly a person, was born
    as the white plant bloomed;
She is the night dream of the spectator,
    incised on the lidless eye;
Woman without face or name that is known
    lives in my house.

Weigh her, measure her, peer for children
in her clouded history; check with Geiger counters
in the click of the doomed leaves and fans.

59

Lost in events the beauty and the grace
    of women;
Ended the age of natural love as the bomb bay opened
On the burned shoulders: she is now
    the memorable one.

From the nightmare to the eye
from the eye to the house
from the house to the heart
enter the dimension of love:

woman of Hiroshima

be merciful to the merciless!

ROBERT HAYDEN

From *Middle Passage*

'Deponent further sayeth The Bella J
left the Guinea Coast
with cargo of five hundred blacks and odd
for the barracoons of Florida:

'That there was hardly room 'tween-decks for half
the sweltering cattle stowed spoon-fashion there;
that some went mad of thirst and tore their flesh
and sucked the blood:

'That Crew and Captain lusted with the comeliest
of the savage girls kept naked in the cabins;
that there was one they called the Guinea Rose
and they cast lots and fought to lie with her:

'That when the Bo's'n piped all hands, the flames
spreading from starboard already were beyond

control, the negroes howling and their chains
entangled with the flames:

"That the burning blacks could not be reached,
that the crew abandoned ship,
leaving their shrieking negresses behind;
that the Captain perished drunken with the wenches:

'Further Deponent sayeth not.'

Pilot   Oh   Pilot   Me

. . . Shuttles in the rocking loom of history,
the dark ships move, the dark ships move,
their bright ironical names
like jests of kindness on a murderer's mouth;
plough through thrashing glister toward
fata morgana's lucent melting shore,
weave toward New World littorals that are
mirage and myth and actual shore.

Voyage through death,
              voyage whose chartings are unlove.

A charnel stench, effluvium of living death,
spreads outward from the hold,
where the living and the dead, the horribly dying,
lie interlocked, lie foul with blood and excrement.

       Deep in the festering hold thy father lies,
       the corpse of mercy rots with him,
       rats eat love's rotten gelid eyes.

       But oh the living look at you
       with human eyes whose suffering accuses you,
       whose hatred reaches through the swill of dark
       to strike you like a leper's claw.

You cannot stare that hatred down
or chain the fear that stalks the watches
and breathes on you its fetid scorching breath;
cannot kill the deep immortal human wish,
the timeless will. . . .

LESLIE WOOLF HEDLEY

Chant for all the People on Earth

Not to forget not to ever forget so long as you live so long as you
love so long as you breathe eat wash walk think see feel read touch
laugh not to forget not to ever forget so long as you know the
meaning of freedom of what lonely nights are to torn lovers so long
as you retain the soul heart of a man so long as you resemble man
in any way in any shape not to forget not to ever forget for many
have already forgotten many have always planned to forget fire fear
death murder injustice hunger gas graves for they have already forgotten and want you to forget but do not forget our beloved species
not to forget not to ever forget for as long as you live carry it with
you let us see it recognize it in each other's face and eyes taste it
with each bite of bread each time we shake hands or use words for
as long as we live not to forget what happened to 6 million Jews to
living beings who looked just as we look men people children girls
women young old good bad evil profound foolish vain happy unhappy sane insane mean grand joyous all dead gone buried burned
not to forget not to ever forget for as long as you live for the earth
will never be the same again for each shred of sand cries with their
cries and our lungs are full of their dying sounds for god was killed
in each of them for in order to live as men we must not forget for
if they are forgotten O if they are forgotten forget me also destroy
me also burn my books my memory and may everything I have ever
said or done or written may it be destroyed to nothing may I become less than nothing for then I do not want even one memory
of me left alive on cold killing earth for life would have no honor
for to be called a man would be an insult—

BARBARA HINCHCLIFFE

A Sunday in the Thirties

On Sunday afternoons we ate a big dinner,
all fourteen of us. And after, the women
talked the dishes clean (trivial women talk of
love and birth and death).
We children went upstairs
and played Monopoly, so we wouldn't have to listen
to Father Coughlin. And the uncles
sat in the parlor and argued. My Uncle Frank—
who lived in New York City and had
a beautiful Mexican mistress who was always trying
to bring him back to the Faith—
he was an atheist. But he used to say,
"All I know about Jesus is,
"he never used a gun;
"he had no use for money;
"he never burned anyone at the stake,
"and by God
"he never turned his back on anybody."

He's dead now. All the uncles
but one are dead, and the aunts.
My cousins live in Levittown
and New Brunswick. I never see them. But
I remember
My Aunt Mary's perfume,
and the ugly rasp of Father Coughlin's voice,
and my mother playing the piano, and
the smell of roast lamb, but mostly
Uncle Frank saying,
"All I know about Jesus—
"he never turned his back on anybody."

CARL WENDELL HINES, JR.

Jazz Poem

yeah here am i
am standing
at the crest of a tallest
hill with a trumpet
in my hand & dark
glasses
on.
    bearded & bereted i proudly stand!
      but there are no eyes to see me.
    i send down cool sounds!
      but there are no ears to hear me.
    my lips they quiver in aether-emptiness!
      there are no hearts to love me.
surely though through night's grey fog mist
of delusion & dream
& the rivers of tears that flow
like gelatin soul-juice
some apathetic bearer of
paranoidic peyote visions (or some
other source of inspiration) shall
    hear the song i play.shall
    see the beard & beret.shall
    become inflamed beyond all hope
with emotion's everlasting fire
& join me
    in
        eternal
            Peace.
& but yet well
who knows?

there he stands. see?
like a black Ancient Mariner his

wrinkled old face so
full of the wearies of living is
turned downward with
closed eyes. his frayed-collar
faded-blue old shirt turns
dark with sweat & the old
necktie undone drops
loosely about the worn
old jacket see? just
barely holding his
sagging stomach in. yeah.
his run-down shoes have
paper in them & his
rough unshaven face shows
pain
in each wrinkle.

but there he stands. in
self-brought solitude head
still down eyes
still closed ears
perked & trained upon
the bass line for
across his chest lies an old
alto saxophone—
supported from his neck by
a wire coat hanger.

gently he lifts it now
to parted lips. see? to
tell all the world that
he is a Black Man. that
he was sent here to preach
the Black Gospel of Jazz.

now preaching it with words of
screaming notes & chords he
is no longer a man. no not even

a Black Man. but (yeah!)
a Bird!—
one that gathers his wings & flies
   high
      high
         higher
until he flies away! or
comes back to find himself
a Black Man
again.

GEORGE HITCHCOCK

From *The Indestructible*

(*For Mariano P. Balgos of the Philippine Hukbalahap*)

   1.

Manila! City of wounds!
Eight years have gone
Yet tonight again, a seaman in a strange port,
I enter your multiple doors
And again you embrace me with your odors and cries.

I walk in the Tondo
And among the sombre houses of the poor
You open your wounds to me:
There I see the sharks' teeth of hunger,
The ulcered sores,
Knives of poverty,
And am pursued by ragged boys
Who sell their sisters to the sergeants.

I come to a certain *nipa* hut.
Here, Mariano,
Though my generals hunt you with warrants
You sit inviolate in the breast of the people.

66

Here the general staff of the landless
Talks of liberty:
Hukbo ng bayan laban sa Japon—
The People's Anti-Japanese Army.
I hear your clear, warm voice, Mariano,
Precise in English
Rippling in Tagalog,
Discuss the alphabet of freedom.
I feel your brown hand in mine,
The hand of a Filipino printer
In that of an American seaman.

"Tell America," you say,
"We remember Rizal
As you remember your Washington
And that cold winter in Delaware.
We have learned from your revolution:
Grant us our own."

Later I walk through the bombed streets
To the Malacañan Palace.
From this house of hungry pockets
Soriano, Roxas, Laurel,
Yesterday Yamashita's dinner-guests,
Emerge with chlorinated teeth
To devour the young doe of liberty.
I see the hand under the table
The airplanes strangely declared surplus
The bribed inspector
The missing shipments of carpets.
For the war is over;
Order is guaranteed,
And property can resume
Its noiseless gnawing on the poor.

On the way back to my ship
I cross the Pasig. Night arrives.
I look down at that river

And think of Crisanto Evangelista
Strangled and drowned by the Japanese.
I gaze at the Pasig
And it is a river of tearing mouths,
Swallower of tears,
Devourer of the bodies
Of my murdered comrades.

Manila! City of wounds!
Eight years have passed and these memories
Should have been interred
In the burial-ground of old travelogues.
But I cannot forget.
Nor shall I ever.

2.

Five thousand miles and as many hopes
Removed, air-conditioned America
Sleeps its beauty sleep.
We live here in the street of lost petals
We live in a house of bones;
Here in this land of fractured statues
We chat of summer and swimming and the latest tenor
While tears fall unnoticed
In our breakfast food.

Voices which cry from underground
Are ignored as indelicate.
Broomstraw
Inksplotch
The cracked bowl
Harass us in our dreams.
Unaware of portents
Unaware of history
Oblivious to hunger
We lift our cups in manicured fingers
And if the child cries in the cellar

Stuff his mouth with rags.
In the eastern sky
Heavens explode like rockets
Yet here in this street of lost petals
The peon's anguish is transmuted
And in suburban cellars
The children of our indifference
Scream like tigers.

Americans, countrymen,
Who of you will see the fist
At the window?

Not you, Belshazzars of the country-club,
Morticians of joy, enemies of the jonquil,
For your eyes, which might have seen,
Are glazed with fear
And your hands
Which might have learned to touch
Have lived too long in gloves.

No, if there are those who will listen,
If there are those
Who will extend recognition to the dawn
Do not look for them in chanceries
But among bakers of bread
Diggers, fabricants, vintners and creators:

Their ears sharpened to the wind
They hear the wind's arrival.
They listen, Mariano.
Do not despair of them.
My country stirs slowly
In its barbiturate slumbers.
But it stirs . . .

And we who traffic in these dreams
Let us be prouder of them

69

Than of myrrh and spices;
For tomorrow's children live in our mind's eye
And should we cease to dream
Will die stillborn.

HERSCHEL HORN

Landscape Near a Steel Mill

Over the books of bricks,
over the vague meanings of dust—
with a taste of leather,
with a rough static of purple, like wine—
entering the empty houses at evening,
the slow circumference of supper hangs out
its banner of striped shadow.

Wallets are closed;
cars start up
like an uprising of lions,
and the furnaces fall into themselves
like a pillow of autumn leaves,
and, with a great sigh of a dead bagpipe,
become in silence, passive sunsets.

How shall I tell you
of all the doors I came upon?
Of the small shredded joys
that cried in paper tears,
and how I saw silence
come down in parachutes of fire?

Yes, all things revolt against
the dying static of sunlight.
Only the bankers are left,
polishing their interest globes

through the long night,
milking their beards
like magicians pulling out quarters
from the combinations of air.

But I shall tell you of the dusty children:
I saw them
scraped through the back of a yawn:
wave-lifted,
their birds flying paper joys,
uncertain in a square of uncertainty,
but echoing in their tinny valleys, galloping hearts.
And I saw hands like
lighted menorahs on the horizon
foreseeing future sunrises,

crying: Fools! Where is our bread?

FRANK HORNE

Resurrection

Some of us
these days
will kneel before altars
resplendent with cloth and gold
redolent with incense
exalted by homage
to a Jew
crucified, dead and buried
—Forgive them, Father, they know not what they do—
who rose from the tomb
with nail holes in His hands and feet
and spear in His side
to teach us
that love conquers all ...

And others of us
will sit around the family table
lift high the cup of wine
and answer four questions
in homage to Jehovah
and Moses
for delivering us in the exodus
out of bondage in Egypt
into the promised land
to live in freedom and light
under the laws of the prophets . . .

And then
there are some of us
—sons and daughters of Ham
—they say
who still toil under the yoke
of bondage and oppression
in a dark and weary land . . .
sometimes we wonder
in anguish—
where is He
that brings love and freedom?
—why hast Thou forsaken me—
where is Moses
to strike off our chains
and lead us into the promised land?

But that still small voice
is thundering louder and louder:
Love ye all men
—yeah even Ross Barnett
    and Faubus and Bull Connor
Love ye all men . . .
and you yourself
press against the yoke
with ballots
and dignity

—and holes in hands and feet
and compassion
even for him
who wields the lash—
—they know not what they do—
and you may save his soul
and theirs that break unleavened bread
—for you were strangers in the land of Egypt
and theirs that eat of His Body and Blood
—love thy neighbor as thyself
and your own
as you impel the world to recall
the triumph of Golgotha
and the glory of love
and the laws of the prophets.

CHARLES HUMBOLDT

Field of Plunder

They send him
Not among the cool flowers
But on that brimming-with-blood
Hard hill, and to the sour shore
Like sideways crawling crabs, claws
Hanging from cliffs of smoke

Not to a calm house—
Trapped by flies in the sand, trod on
By the monster sun, wind made of dust
Shutting his eyes and mouth, buzzing
In his breath

Not riding home
From the beach, the show, the game, the park
In the bluegold air, reclined in speech

Because of the day and evening and night
So long and graced with acts of love

But by the burnt walls crying and
In the dry river biting stones, learning
To walk in the shade of clanking iron
To whirl in circles when guns cough
To run forward and backward
Through the chalk gully, toward the split tree

A dream of love covered by snowing death
No time, no place for the stars of heaven
And flowers of long walks

A dream of flying flesh, shrubs of white fume
A plan of scorched bones and scattered teeth
A bell crying bong, bong, bong
Over those who never did him wrong.

The masters of the hunt
Cried for a wounded paw
If a falcon fell from the sky
Someone would have died
Of sorrow for that symbolic bird

But those who send him
Wait, behind the hills
Beaked and blinking, till the sound of death
Tells them to soar, and now they hop
On the bleached horror, the cracked bell
The smell of man delighting them, as they
Pick profit on the field that curses them.

JOE JOHNSON

Judeebug's Country

Twilight glitters on the fragmented glass.
It condescends to scratch the ancient wall
Casting a fetid shadow in a hallway scented
with murmured conversations . . . loitering with broken
mailboxes ajar on expectant hinges.

The shadows are jarred by Judeebug
A black little . . . A bad little . . . motherhugger
He is the thunder splintering stairs hastening
The tenement's demurring death.
Judeebug, Judeebug, a black little, a bad little . . .
Motherhugger whose world is the block beneath unpadded
U.S. Keds, whose pants a Blumstein special, one dollar
Ninety-eight . . . a dollar ninety-eight plus taxes

        Can't jive the wind   Can't jive the wind

The sky a black woman's bosom bursting blues, brooding black

Caddys pass, babies cry, chicken frys
Daddy's choir sings, Michaux's flags wave

Judeebug . . . Judeebug your dreams can't jive the wind!
The sky a soiled cotton swob against indifferent grey . . . Judeebug
They cry over your vacant hands . . . They bathe your wounds
In pity's bourgeois salve
Don't pray, sit, wade, or lay-in, Don't teach him to read
The warped syntax of the white page,
Don't take the note that he holds warm in his throat,
Let him hit: "Oh say can you see" . . . Oh, say can you see!
Judeebug, a bad little, black little—motherhugger
Whose dreams won't jive the wind,
¾ man and the Parthenon is crumblin'

KAY JOHNSON

A Defiant Song

...Sorrow
tempers the heart to a compass point.
When all is lost, then I begin.
When hope is gone, the marrow of my bones
    begins to sing.
I ride wild the winds of torment,
soar, like a laughing bird
    through the harm meant.

Strike me freedom on the anvil of your hate!
Unleash necessity to love, to smile,
To wait the common cage of brotherhood
to snare me, like a vice.

I'm not your kind, cannot be wooed,
    by else but blood.
And I must fall, like homing birds
    into the sun.

LEROI JONES

Contract

(For the destruction and rebuilding of Paterson)

Flesh, and cars, tar, dug holes beneath stone
a rude hierarchy of money, band saws cross out
music, feeling. Even speech, corrodes.
                I came here
from where I sat boiling in my veins, cold fear
at the death of men, the death of learning, in

76

cold fear, at my own. Romantic vests of same death
blank at the corner, blank when they raise their fingers

Criss the hearts, in dark flesh staggered so marvelous
are their lies. So complete, their mastery, of these
stupid niggers. Loud spics kill each other, and will not

make the simple trip to Tiffany's. Will not smash their stainless
heads, against the simpler effrontery of so callous a code as gain.

You are no brothers, dirty woogies, dying under dried rinds, in
  massa's
droopy tuxedos. Cab Calloways of the soul, at the soul's juncture, a
music, they think will save them from our eyes. (In back of the
  terminal

where the circus will not go. At the backs of crowds, stooped and
  vulgar
breathing hate syllables, unintelligible rapes of all that linger in
our new world. Killed in white fedora hats, they stand so mute at
  what

whiter slaves did to my fathers. They muster silence. They pray at
  the
steps of abstract prisons, to be kings, when all is silence, when all
is stone. When even the stupid fruit of their loins is gold, or something
else they cannot eat.

AARON KURTZ

From *Behold the Sea*

... They got you last night.
I saw you clubbed.
I recognized the nightsticks: they were thorny twigs

77

From the tree from where I saw
your brother lynched.
They felt the same as those they used
on my Father in Maidenek.

I saw a boot step on your throat last night:
it was the same boot that stepped on my young sister's throat.

I saw you shot last night.
I saw the gun: it was the gun they used
on my brother in Dachau . . .

I saw clear white, pure white
from White House to the Ku Klux Klan's white robes
and the white gardenias in the lapels of justice—
white guns booming in Mississippi courthouses.
white guns on campuses proclaiming
white law of love and brotherhood . . .

I saw Christ flog you on the chain gang.
I saw Christ put the torch to your brother on a heartbroken tree.
I saw Christ torture you on Times Square.
(That wasn't Christ at all, of course—it was Judas raving he was
    Christ, with thumb on trigger).
I saw your children chased from a white open hydrant on a hot day
    in Alexandria. I wanted to cry,
but would not dare
after I heard your mothers crying from a million
smoke holes in the black belt.
I heard the wise old trees of Georgia cry the cry of your lynched
    sons.
I saw the scabrous,
filthy walls of Harlem cry the cry of your clean heart . . .

One day at dawn
I saw the toppled white tombstones of your great
rise and grow

taller than
the tallest lynch trees of your land.
    I saw Paul
standing on the beach—singing
across the sea
I heard his mighty voice, tragic thunder of
man's heart, rearing through the waves. I thought it was
the roaring sea, singing
to our brother, singing to
our might.

—translated from the Yiddish by the author.

PETER LA FARGE

Vision of a Past Warrior

I have within me such a dream of pain
That all my silver horseman hopes rust still,
Beyond quick silver mountains,
On the plain,
The buffalo are gone,
None left to kill,

I see the plains grow blackened with that dawn,
No robes for winter warmth
No meat to eat,
The ghost white buffalos' medicine gone,
No hope for Indians then,
I see defeat.

Then there will be changes to another way,
We will fight battles that are legends long.
But of all our glory
None will stay,
Who will remember
That I sang this song.

79

CARL LARSEN

The Plot to Assassinate the Chase Manhattan Bank

To assassinate the Chase Manhattan Bank
Is not as easy as you'd think.
I walked in, see, and yelled "Kings-X!"
and saw what looked like great machines
come rumbling to a halt, and I thought,
fine—I'm halfway home. Then God rose from
the Office of the President,
a little miffed, I think, and said,
"What's on your mind?"
"I came up from the Coast," I said,
"to blow this pad to—if you will
excuse my pun—to Kingdom Come."
"You can't do that, my Son," he said,
and that's how I knew he was God,
although he looked a great deal
like John Wayne. "You wouldn't want,"
he said, "to do away with this—"
and from each teller's cage, a flock
of rainbow doves flew up, and settled
near the roof. "Put down your bomb,
let's have a talk," he said, and smiled.
I laid aside the bomb and followed him
into his office, and sat down.
"The Proletariat demands," I said,
"You cease this madness"; And he
smiled again. I saw he had a golden tooth.
"Some for the glories of this world,"
God said, then showed a picture of his family,
and then his house, a nice split-level
place up in the Bronx. His wife,

80

a pleasant-looking woman,
had inscribed it: "Love, In God We Trust".
He wiped away the tears that gathered
in the corners of his steely eyes,
choked back a sob, and called The Fuzz.
Inside a minute, forty cops popped from
the walls and drawers, came running from
the vault where God kept love, and
clamped the irons around my feet.
"Now Jean Valjean," God shouted,
gaining his composure, "now you'll
face the rack!" I pleaded it was all
a joke. I said I'd be a good li'l boy
and stay home playing with my spiders
if he'd let me go. But his bit was not
forgiveness, and they locked me in
a dungeon full of nasty things he had
discarded, like the stars,
and sea-foam, and the earth.

DENISE LEVERTOV

From *Matins*

2.

... The authentic! I said
rising from the toilet seat.
The radiator in rhythmic knockings
spoke of the rising steam.
The authentic, I said
breaking the handle of my hairbrush as I
brushed my hair in
rhythmic strokes: That's it,
that's joy, it's always
a recognition, the known

appearing fully itself, and
more itself than one knew.

3.

The new day rises
as heat rises,
knocking in the pipes
with rhythms it seizes for its own
to speak of its invention—
the real, the new-laid
egg whose speckled shell
the poet fondles and must break
if he will be nourished . . .

4.

Stir the holy grains, set
the bowls on the table and
call the child to eat.

While we eat we think,
as we think an undercurrent
of dream runs through us
faster than thought
towards recognition.
Call the child to eat,
send him off, his mouth
tasting of toothpaste, to go down
into the ground, into a roaring train
and to school.

His cheeks are pink
his black eyes hold his dreams, he has left
forgetting his glasses.

Follow down the stairs at a clatter
to give them to him and save
his clear sight.

Cold air
comes in at the street door.

5.

The authentic! It rolls
just out of reach, beyond
running feet and
stretching fingers, down
the green slope and into
the black waves of the sea.
Speak to me, little horse, beloved,
tell me
how to follow the iron ball,
how to follow through to the country
beneath the waves
to the place where I must kill you and you step out
of your bones and flystrewn meat
tall, smiling, renewed,
formed in your own likeness. . . .

JACK LINDEMAN

Lament for the Frontiers of the Empire

[All that has the face of rage and does not raise its
voice. Acquiescence lights up the face. Refusal gives
it beauty.   —RENE CHAR]

Abracadabra, and here I am
in a land majoritied by the amber skinned,
for whom white is the fiendish extreme
in the spectrum of various horrors.
Not with a smile of heavily grenaded
missionary phrases do I take the bomber's enemy
for friend. Morsel for thought,

83

I have lugged you across obese topography
without refrigeration for the mouths of the hungry.
Yet nothing but pain
   do my countrymen lavish
      upon the bones of the scrawny,
         philanthropy being their mode of deception.
Let the helpless scream
and a thousand monks of alien gods go up in smoke,
for the noise of tongues will diminish
beneath burial tons of fallow alluvial.
I will lift weights from my conscience
   with the strength of words.
O inertia of minds,
    why do you acquiesce
       in the sonorous slogans of turning wheels
         that grind the pagodas of the human heart
            into dust for asphalt turnpikes?
I drift thru calendars in an aluminum punt
joining hands with the funeral processions
   of companionless mourners
beneath the gold of the sun's shadow.

WALTER LOWENFELS

From *Letter to the President*

... What weather of shelters
   our own or anybody's analogs—
feeds down the icecaps to computers
   its song of fallout
      this spring?

What crawl of cobalt
   cracks the blood count with bells,
dissolves the crystals
   and divides the lovebirds in the laboratories
      from the dead?

Grasses that hold footprints of ants,
    neutrons where the ladybugs go,
all the jets—missiles—milk and roses
    swing an orbit of rockets
the human ear echoes when it hears
    in any isotope
or lover's touch
    the song of megatons
this spring. . . .

This is the time of the limited suicide when I keep you
    from killing yourself with machine guns and bayonets,
because I have a 100-megaton bomb produced by the Snake God
    who doesn't care how you get there—or in how many
installments as long as the national debt passes away in
    time for another generation of shock troops to renew
        the charge.
It then becomes essential to know precisely how crazy
    the other computer is getting to be
if you want to keep the edge of deterrence open at your end.
Also, at what microsecond of the day he reaches his median,
    so you can adjust your early dew warning system to
                his ups and downs,
Under these circumstances, our neighbors lived a purely
                normal life
    the birthrate increased, the death rate declined,
    the 9% unemployment got built-in for life,
and everybody lived happily in the suburbs of forever after.

            Meanwhile
there are enough megatons in the world to kill
everybody 12 times.

    And the faintly disbelieving edges
    disappear behind the oakleaf
    where the shell on the beach bends
and the lie disappears just around the

                        corner drug store

85

And the credibility of our deterrence kits
                                will not save us
from the 11th Commandment:
    Thou Shalt Not Overkill.

RICHARD LYONS

Goodbye the Office

Goodbye the office, goodbye the chatters,
Goodbye the typewriters, goodbye the fac-
Tory mind, the tabula rasa filed and lined
With decimal precisions, now that the shellac
Sun fallows the spring-down evening, shatters

The upward-sky with clouds and abstract lines
Empiercing dull imaginations, at-
Rophied of practice, embarrassing and DP'ed.
Pencil spring, as muddy as the Platte,
Flows down the *hooihut* of white designs.

Goodbye the deskrows, goodbye fluorescent
Unseasoned light. The afternoon is flav-
Ored out with peavine energy, the shut-
Warm, spring-toward season of streetlight sav-
Ory night. This is the green and crescent

Season of fever. Through traffic of hot glass
Toward supper and cigarettes and the ev-
Ening paper. Such as it is, escape.
And eponymous Pan, to those who still believe,
In the outside sound of kids on the uncut grass.

WILLIAM J. MARGOLIS

Telegram

IN MISSISSIPPI COLD LILIES
STICK UP LIKE LIES AGAINST
MILES OF FLAGPOLES—TELEPHONE WIRES
ARE BRIGHT IN SUMMER SUNSHINE
AND NO AMOUNT OF CROSSES
CAN OBLITERATE THEIR WEATHERING.

LOVE

GOD

JAMES BOYER MAY

Reflection after Empire

Bitumen flanges of this living track
burn Congo flames, low brown in color,
painingly by blacked crowds of banyan trees
seeing how purposely resentments spread
to Burma. Darkest continent won't hold
such fires, nor white denials quench them
in mid-ocean; for every isthmus shorts
the circuits with steel strictures.

Not red names of movements, but
their common knowledge of rapacities
enduing hatted bosses of
those bareheaded gangs which
built these roads.

STUART MCCARRELL

The Assassinations 1963

A dark day. The rain in Washington, the little feet of death.
Some of the same molecules that chilled the heat of Xerxes,
of fabled Khans, blond conquerors and black, martyrs and fools.
Nothing helps against this tasteless, unclouded brew.
Jack Kennedy, rich and clever.
Jack Kennedy, young, adored in Dallas sun.
Hours later in this desperate sea. Sinking forever.
"Call no man fortunate until he is dead." The first poet said it.
The very last will be able to add—not one word.
I, with the rest, sorrow for you. But I will not lie.
Your virtues and your flaws were intertwined and balanced even.
No rich boy without some special suffering feels
the loneliness of the poor, the worry,
the danger in every week, each task, each smile
returned or turned aside—the swish of forces centered far away.
Jefferson and the second Roosevelt were such men.
But if you were not it hardly matters.
Such flame to transcend class, to pitch love disinterested
on the people and their sweaty haloed hair,
is rare as the albino elephants they war over in the East.
But you were young, full of courage and wit,
playing the game you loved for the cheers you loved.
Your death had an honor of its own.
But not martyrdom.
His was not martyrdom either. Not consciously.
He knew all the things you didn't.
The belly tearing anger. The quick sympathy.
The quicker hate. May God save, or spare a little
the thin skinned poor. Such blows
as your class lays on them casually:
the falsified service records,
the guttural lies, the bone breaking fists of southern cops,

the whining lies of TV "historians,"
turn them in pain all their life.
Throw them after a slow or quick death to crows.
Unmourned, while a black orgy rages for you.
O we are two nations. Always. Always,
Until the day the people retake the plunder.
But now, for a while yet, I write from the underground.
I speak for him, the tongueless, the drugged, the deceived.
For until that day, then no man will inherit mansions
and another rat running slums, righteous rage, usually impotent
will gut the best sons of the poor,
turn the worst into these savage murderous sheriffs
striking down their brothers for small dirty jobs,
and leave your curly brothers as now,
arrogant horsemen blind with sun, laughing and casual,
defending their privilege, their patterns
not with swords or danger to themselves
but by throwing trinkets to the natives,
small dirty jobs to those who'll take them.

MICHAEL MCCLURE

Fidelio

Charming bearded singer! Make the beast's tune
that precedes the triumphal ending of mankind's symphony.
We hold our breath & listen to the roar.
Your tongue is ruby meat and vibrates a new melody
of new virtue to the starving and poor.
Eyes are mild within your lion's face.
A finish will come for the old lore;
and with your clean arm and paw
the clotted massy dishes will be swept
and the world
left as pure as an old dark table
covered by a gleaming linen cloth

so stark and warm
it may reflect the high points of your song.

BUT BEWARE OF THE EAGLE WITH WHITE HEAD!

Watch it closely with your dark-starred
mammal eyes.
The hopes of freedom are with you. . . .
and opposed are the lies!

THOMAS MCGRATH

From *Letter to an Imaginary Friend*

. . . Blessed, blessed

Oh blessed

Blessed be changing day and night and the old far-ranging
Starry signs of the loved, continual, surprising seasons;
Blessed be dark and light, blessed be freezing and burning,
Blessed be the gold fur of the He-sun and the moons-down shine
of the great
Bold, changing, Woman queening the wild night-sky;
Blessed be the metric green confusion of the crowding, cold, es-
tranging and inconstant sea;
Blessed be the stay-at-home land, the rocking mountains under the
loose loud sky;
Blessed be speech and silence;
Blessed be the blood hung like a bell in my body's branching tree;
Blessed be dung and honey;
Blessed be the strong key of my sex in her womb,
The electric bird of desire, trapped in the locked-room mysteries of
country charm;
Blessed be my writing hand and arm and the black lands of my
secret heart.

90

Blessed be the birds of the high forest hung on a wing of song;
Blessed be the long sin of the snake and his fangs blessed;
Blessed be the fishing bear in his shine and fury;
Blessed be flower and weed: sheet, spike, rhizome, raceme, sepal
and petal;
The blued-out wildlings; metallic, green marsh-hiders shy; high-
climbers, low-rooters.
Beast, bird, tree, stone, star: blessed, blessed.

And blessed be friends and comrades:
Blessed be Rolfe in his dark house and the hearts of friends.
Blessed, by the loud continuous sea: Naomi.
Blessed on their mountains under the enshrouding shine of the
spent stars' light: Don and Charlie:
With their wives, children, heirs and assigns.
Blessed, blessed
In the waste lots and the burning cities of man's estate,
Fishers by still streams, hunters on the hard hills, singers, dreamers
and makers:
Blessed be all friends
With their wives, husbands, lovers, sons, daughters, heirs and
assigns
Forever.

Blessed be the fighters:
The unknown angry man at the end of the idiot-stick with his
dream of freedom;
Jawsmiths and soap boxers, gandy-dancers setting the high iron
Toward the ultimate Medicine Hat: blessed, blessed.
Blessed the agitator; whose touch makes the dead walk;
Blessed the organizer; who discovers the strength of wounds;
Blessed all fighters.

Blessed be my loves: in the wreckage of morning light,
In the high moon-farms, in the horny hot night of the dry, gone
summers,
In the heat of lust and thunder of the noon sheets—
Blessed be flesh and voice, blessed forever;

Blessed thy belly and legs;
Blessed be thy woman's warmth in this human winter.

Blessed, blessed

                                Oh blessed
Blessed be Marian,
All ways the honey flesh of this girl with light on her shoulder
Oh blessed, blessed!

And blessed now be all children:
Hunters come through the space warp, waking
Into their unmade world under the sign of our outlaw fire;
Blessed their hopes and confusions;
Blessed their deeps and darks
Their friends and lovers, heirs and assigns forever.

And blessed, blessed, blessed, blessed
Be my wife and love, and her body's being:
Green song of the double-meaning sea;
Tree of my dreamless bird, unsleeping quarry of seamless
Light; feathery river of the sensual continent, unseasonal rain
Under the riven sky of my dry thunderstruck night-side heart
Unending lightning. . . .

                              Oh blessed!

And blessed myself and myselves . . .
Turning homeward . . .
                     under the waking shapes of the rain. . . .
Blessed.

Now, toward midnight, the rain ends.
The flowers bow and whisper and hush;
                      the clouds break
And the great blazing constellations rush up out of the dark
To hang in the flaming North. . . .

Arcturus, the Bear, the Hunter
Burning. . . .

Now, though the Furies come, my furious Beast,
I have heard the Laughter,
And I go forward from catastrophe to disaster
Indifferent: singing:
My great ghosts and the Zodiac of my dead
Swing round my dream.

Star-shine steady over this house where I sit writing this down—
2714 Marsh Street—
                              Drifting toward Gemini. . . .
Night, pure crystal,
                    coils in my ear like
                              song . . .

EVE MERRIAM

Block Party

On the corner, right angular, facing the park
The Christian Science church, its granite base
Grimed by the city street, engraven "Purity";
Further down, the Free Synagogue chanting,
Flights of angelic pigeons and the gold-rushed plane to California.
Rising prices at the A&P where the women roll their groundmeat
    menus home;
Baby carriages, children on skates, laundry handtruck,
Grocer's boy pedaling, police prowl car,
Elephant vans, postman humped with bills and dues,
Dogs walking their owners,
someone moving out, his alter ego in,
So any day wheels on all motion and commotion.

The cigar-store owner with the gray newspaper skin
Shrugs at his unsold pile.

93

"I didn't order so many. The big dealers tell me what I have to
  take."
Cashes a relief check, notarizes disaster.
Rings up a deposit bottle of coke.
His wife shrills at the penny youngsters banging the door,
Popsicle-dripping over the silkslick magazines,
But her eyes give her away, a tune sweet and true.
She sighs: "May they never grow up to go to war again."

The garbage cans clatter: Keep Your City Clean.
Wrappered housewives undo their mops
On the vacant lot next door.
From her crowded vacant window, the penthouse woman.
The Irish elevator runner gabs with the Negro doorman,
Leaves him to eat his lunch alone.

Delivery to the duplex
Where the advertising executive, married mistress, and baby mink
  daughter
All are analyzing their dreams.
Basement-stooped, the tailor knots his threadbare flesh.
May the heart hold.

Some final passion has made the early edition,
And the sign reads anew "Room to let."
No story in the widow dying in the arms of her
Unpaid gas and electric bill.
The sculptor seeks a definitive curve in clay,
The writer woos his notebook,
The painter goes elsewhere for material.

The day is sunlight in winter, and the kid sister takes courage,
Steps out of line for a minute, talks back to her older brother:
"You're not the boss of the whole wide world"!

Twilight turns on,
The bar-and-grill proclaims neon Hallelujah,
The victor in the televised wrestling bout.

The facsimile French restaurant douses winey sauce
Over the single woman and her lending library nights,
Over the older man and his young companion
St. Christopher pendants calming their throbbing Tahitian shirts.

The separate lights go on in all the separate rooms.
Was that someone at the door?
No, it's only the Negro maid.
I thought I heard someone at the door.
Only the old man home again from work.
Are you sure there's no one at the door?
Only, murmurs the adolescent, lonely me.

And now it is night,
Black-bordering night of the official proclamation
Commanding us each to deeper separateness.
All-out for more unliving.
The State of National Emergency declares
There is an Emperor and he does wear clothes;
Windows are not for a view of the street,
But peephole spying.

Oh let us take shelter not out of catastrophe
Playing prone to the make-believe air raid warden,
Huddling back to back under pretended attack from un-sky.
What warning, what wedding will unite us
So that a river of light will run leaping through the walls
Unfolding our purse-fisted hands to open palms,
Lifting us higher than the stars, level with one another's eyes,
Seeing ourselves beautifully workday common and Sunday varied,
My neighborhood block unbossed, replanned
With doors, windows, and the whole world opening wide?

MAY MILLER

The Last Warehouse

The roaches are winning, Mr. Exterminator.
They breathe back at you the poisoned delirium
Through which you see the man in bug
And mimicked our own clocked ending
When they go belly-whopping in death dust
Or flipping on their backs wiggle
The edge of doom with stubborn legs.

You admit twelve hundred kinds of these—
The female bodies satin-slick with eggs,
The eyes in bulging vengeance
To measure man's naked dread
Against their own disdain.
Toss a brazen penny to decide;
Heads, they win; tails, we die.

Douse them until in the flush of ruin rain
They are saturated with their decrease
That we who abnegate survival laws
May squeeze an effort to defeat
Their plundering the last warehouse.

J. M. MURPHY

The Flagmakers

When the flagmakers heard the news from their man in D.C.
that Alaska and Hawaii had been admitted to the Union
they yelled hip hip hooray and played
ring around the rosy bust of Henry Ford
to a hi-fi version of *The Stars & Bars*

*F*orever. Next day
they drove in Lincolns to the flag factory
where they broke out vats of crimson Eau de Vie
hoarded patiently in combat helmets
by survivors of Anzio, Iwo, Inchon, who had planned
to use it for ink to write their congressmen
but never found the time, being free
and busy making money—which Eau de Vie
army surplus after VJ Day
sold for a song to the flag company.
for a bloodsucking song to the flag company.
And they brought out bolts of fine blue cloth
once worn by Union men in the Civil War
and bolts of good white cloth from cotton picked
by tenant farmers in the deep
south where labor's black and cheap.
So the flagmakers said the word and then and there
the blue was chopped into squares, the red
congealed into peppermint stripes, and the white
froze into bars, hard bars, or was fed
to the GE Electronic Snip 'n' Sew Competitive-Priced Starmaker
guaranteed to produce ten thousand cutrate stars a minute.
They turned out 628,643 fifty-star spangled banners
(all exactly alike) the first week: one for each
citizen of Alaska and Hawaii. Their man in D.C.
got his face on the front of *Time*, a fat
incentive check, the Silver Star, a pat
on the ass from Senator Snorr,
and a trip to Berlin to do PR
for the Third World War.

97

HOWARD McCORD

Two There Are I Wish to Celebrate

The weather was better than you would expect
God to provide: the clouds conversed,
The sky was no abnormal blue.
The windward approach was clear.

Baggy birds with men inside, hunched
At a table, praying coffee to calm
That tumult of the gut, to lull the insides
Back to small and still.

The engines' roar began.

It is known that Major Eatherly
Reported no more than the weather
He did not urge the Enola Gay
To spill her fire.

He spoke calmly and in ignorance.
Captain Van Pelt heard his voice
And said himself the date: August
The Sixth.

So counts man.
When it was done, Van Pelt, who would
Have been an obstetrician, cried
That his hands could gently pull
No children to that sum
If all his years, he dipped
Into the womb of every woman
He should ever see

Not so many babes
As burned that day

Claude Eatherly most sanely
Went most mad.

No man can do more than he
That wakes his empty bed
With eyes as horror as the light

How is it that the rest sleep easily?

You and me

MYRON O'HIGGINS

Sunset Horn

While you cry Victory! or Surrender!
Turn these figures in the head,
Clean impersonal round numbers,
Ordered inventory of the dead.

Regard these slender nines and ones;
These trailing threes and fives; these fours and sevens, bent and
    angular;
Delicately drawn, divided into ranks by commas,
Staggered down the page in regimented squads and columns:
These are our mute effigies, trim and shining,
Passing in review . . .
                        O Drummer, obediently we come,
Down through the assassin's street,
The company of death in splendid array! . . .

But leave us to the terrible fields.
Yours is the pomp of brasses, the counterfeit peace, the dynasty of
    lies . . .

We are but dabs of flesh blown to the cliffs,
Or ragged stumps of legs that moved too slowly toward the brush.
And our song: we joined no swelling harmony of voices.
Those final incoherent sounds we made;
Those startled oaths that bubbled through the blood bogged in our
    throats;
That last falsetto cry of terror;
Were a jagged threnody, swallowed whole and drowned in
    cacophonic floods.
This was our sunset horn . . .
Let these be added with the spoils for quick division!
Set these down in sharp italics on the page
For scholars' documents!

Raise no vain monuments; bury us down!
Our power is manifest in other glory;
Our flesh in this contested slope of ground.
There is no more but these, a legacy, a grim prediction . . .
Let the scent and sounds of death go limp
And flounder in the valleys and the streets.
And for those crafty ones—those who speak our names in brief
    professional remembrance
To garner votes and profits, or practice quick extortion—
Let other music find their ears.
And give them for a souvenir this clown's disguise
Of swastikas and Roman standards, of scythes and suns and dollar
    signs . . .
One day the rest of you will know the meaning of annihilation.
And the hills will rock with voltage;
And the forests burn like a flaming broom;
And the stars explode and drop like cinders on the land.
And these steel cities where no love is—
You shall see them fall and vanish in a thunder of erupting suns!
O you shall know; and in that day, traveler, O in that day
When the tongues confound, and breath is total in the horn,
Your Judas eyes, seeking truth at last, will search for us
And borrow ransom from this bowel of violence!

JOEL OPPENHEIMER

From 17–18 April, 1961

        . . . remember, america
eugene debs said he would not
lead you into paradise if he could,
because if he could lead you in,
someone else could lead you out, that
was the text you ought to have
listened to, that was the text you
ought to have believed, instead you
bought a world free for democracy
and you bought a return to normalcy,
and you bought a new deal, and four
freedoms (freedoms you might only
have, anyhow, if you look deep inside
yourself where all freedom is to be
found, and not with rockwell hands so
carefully and badly drawn . . . and then
america they will be unnumbered, un
countable freedoms inside you, america),
america yes the square deal and the
new frontier. . . .

      and yet even so there were
signs all along, the big money
burned benedict arnold and he went
to the bigger money then, the big
money took ethan allen and battered
him down, he chose to sit out the
rest of the war, the big money did
not like what mr paine might say,
and he paid for it too, the big money
fought and beat or bought all of them one
way or another, and some they killed . . .
let's not talk about it, the big money

101

is always there, you were supposed to
be bigger than it, america, sometimes
you almost were too, think of andy
jackson fighting and beating mr
biddle's bank, and better yet, two
terms later mr tyler in spite of his
politics came to feel some of the
greatness of america in the president's
seat and would not restore mr biddle's bank.

but oh how many battles have you lost
for each one you won, america, are they
enough to balance out? i think they are
not, finally i am through with it, with
the american dream, a dream than ran through
all my ancestors who fought here for you
america, and i still grew up a jew in
yonkers new york, forced constantly to
blurt out historical fact, great grandpa
carried a minie ball in his leg i would
say, and feeling the sickness in me when
haym salomon was praised in ninth grade
and all this shit, and still i was a
jew in yonkers new york, america, don't
misunderstand me, this a man can put up
with, this a man can learn to live with,
roll it off his back sometimes, until the
breakthrough comes, but this is only part
of what is bothering me now, this is, in
the end, my own problem in my own soul, but
the problem in your soul is that 63 years
after mr mckinley we are still fugging
around with dreams of empire, we still
cannot bear to let people work out their
own destiny, we still cannot believe in
keeping our hands off, we have forgotten
we once carried a flag into battle that
read don't tread on me, we think we have

the right to step anywhere, we are free,
and therefore every other man is beneath
us to be trod upon. i will not do it,
america, i will fight my own battles with
my own enemies, but i will not have the
police and the cia and the fbi and whatever
other force you dream of america protect
me from my own heaven or hell. . . .

RAYMOND PATTERSON

In Time of Crisis

You are the brave who do not break
In the grip of the mob when the blow comes straight
To the shattered bone; when the sockets shriek;
When your arms lie twisted under your back.

Good men holding their courage slack
In their frightened pockets see how weak
The work that is done—and feel the weight
Of your blood on the ground for their spirits' sake;

And build their anger, stone on stone—
Each silently, but not alone.

IRENE PAULL

To Bill Heikkila, American

(Whom they tried to make a man without a country.
Given at his funeral in San Francisco May 10, 1960)

I am the wind
I am the northern wind that blows across the Arrowhead to you,
  Bill Heikkila

Across the land of ten thousand lakes
And the big sea waters.
I am the wind that whines in the open pits of Nashwauk and
    Hibbing and Coleraine
And blows upon the red dust of the Mesaba
I am the wind in the hoarse voices of the ships at Allouez, Duluth
    Split Rock and Castle Danger
And all the ports of call of the Unsalted Sea.
You've heard me purring in the birches of the Big Fork, the Gun
    Flint and Echo Trail
Over the bunkhouses of the lumberjacks
I am the same wind that howled like a wounded wolf on the winter
    prairies.
I come to you bearing the perfume of the first spring crocus
The buds of lilacs
I come stroking the grey fur of the pussywillows.
I am the wind that breathes your father's name in the underground
    coal pits of Hanna, Wyoming
In the blast furnaces of the Monongahela
As I shall breathe your name forever in the Arrowhead
You live, Bill Heikkila, You live.
You live in the timbers of the mine shafts
You live in the rock between the furrows
You live in the stumps of cedar
And burnt over popple
On the road you cut to the Pale Face River.
The land nourishes men and men nourish the land
You have seeped to the roots of Minnesota
Like the melted snows of 54 winters.
I shall breathe your name, Bill Heikkila, among the jackpine
I shall mingle your dust with the red ore of the Mesaba
And where the long boats load at Allouez
And the fog horn warns them off the rocks at Castle Danger.

I am the wind that carried your shouts
I have spread them like pollen.
I am the wind that lifted your banners
I have scattered their seed

They shall blossom again on city streets
In another season.
You live, Bill Heikkila, you live
I am the Northern wind.

ANNE PETERS

From *Kevin O'Culihain*
Zorro Tio of the Andes
Exile

...Ah, well! In the great Empire of all
    I shall know the why
    That fixed for me to be out away,
    A shawn putting up poles
    Over the spines of the Andes
    To carry the wires
    To put lights in towns and huts
    And power the mines.

    And now
    With the frost come over my fox-red hair—
    I'm known across the Bolivian plateaus,
    Height upon height, by mule drivers,
    Ancianos and workers
    As Zorro Tio—Fox Uncle—
    Boss of Don Rudolf's Mines.

    But I was reared back there
    Where Great-Grandad's thatched house
    Is founded on the down-sloped hills
    Tucked between hedges, face to the sea,
    Weathering the noon sun
    And the mist-laden winds
    And I would go there now:
    Yes, now! To Ardaghcloe,

As Yeats, God rest him, went
And wrote hushed lines about
The isle within our island . . .

O Ochone! 'Tis the beat of your seas
Emerald and endless and full of whip
And the weep of your rains
That sings, rings and lives in me always
In spite of this dry-grit-in-teeth
Snow height brood of abyss-built towers
And the sight of your hills
With the lambs muzzling cosy in the heather
And the red, red deer—
Offspring of the wild red deer
That King Malachy hunted for food—
The same walking safe, without fear
Like the children playing ball
In your green, green greens
And the parks in the spitting breeze
And the sheen of the sun
And the peace, even in the dark
And porter-smelling pubs,
And the old, quiet and complaining,
And the rest, groaning or dreaming,
And the sea bordering you all
That keeps the love inside,
Not fearing never catching a glimpse of you.
Sure in the finish of length waiting for me
When lifted and healed in the clean clear
Won't you be the more loved there
For the forces tearing at me now? . . .

WILLIAM PILLIN

Miserere

I will endow you with a false glow
ghetto
or say that only poets and seers
died in your ashes.
Many mourn the scholars and dreamers,
the beautiful innocent talented victims.
I will spare my tears for the
loudmouthed unhappy conniving
Jews
the usurious lenders,

tuberculous hunchbacked
scum of the ghettos (the sweepings of Europe).
For them I will weep,
                        for the whores
pale in the doorways, for the spiderous tradesman
with his false measures
                        and for the grey sparrows
hopping about the winters of Poland
                        the grief of whose eyes
went up in thin smoke like a final prayer.

For them I will weep, I want them returned,
the dwellers of dives, brothels and taverns.
I want them
back as they were, piteous, ignoble,
instead of these grey ashes
that like a winding sheet settle on shivering Europe.

ALAN PLANZ

Conjecture for a Short Mechanic

I remember your dream, born of the hawkless hills,
    you inscribed in the greasepit
        wall with screwdriver and palette of sludge
—your car, your baby, shark-snouted, channeled, chromed,
                hopped up,
    made delicately like a woman from the bone out.

Still, it never got you laid: too full of bugs, cranky
    to run for long, and
        you never won a race. Well, you wanted something
                 more—what
you wouldn't say. Each night you ran the hills.
    Finally opening body and soul
        thru hard steel on them. So
    I'll never know. So
    what.

Yet the winter hills are just right for traveling.
    The road breaks out
        of hill after hill, thru hardwoods into pines,
then up past the timberline, under the stars, the horizon
                falling away

for miles in the cold still air,
    the engine climbing into full torque
and the body singing
        as though wolves howled from extinct caves in the
                bloodstream.

WILLIAM J. POMEROY

Beyond Barriers

Immured in time as bees in amber were,
That in a moment of winged beauty drowned,
Caught in an attitude of flight, then bound
Transparent in their prison forever,
We who were taken midway in the beat
Of hearts and held, suffer a stilled moment,
The arms at curve, the limbs in passion bent,
The captured kiss remaining incomplete:
And if some long era afterward
The fumbling hands of hunters find our trace,
Let it be said that what was here interred
Was beauty, wrenched from its own rightful place,
And frozen impotently in time's prism
That makes a lovely thing of cataclysm.

ISHMAEL REED

The Ghost in Birmingham

The only Holy Ghost in Birmingham is Denmark Vesey's Holy
Ghost, brooding, moving in and out of things. No one notices the
figure in antique cloak of the last century, haunting the pool
games, talking of the weather with a passerby, attending mass
meetings, standing guard, coming up behind each wave of protest,
reloading a pistol. No one notices the antique figure in shabby
clothing, moving in and out of things—rallies of moonshine
gatherings—who usurps a pulpit and preaches a fire sermon,
plucking the plumage of a furious hawk, a sparrow having passively
died, moving in and out of chicken markets, watching sparrow
habits become hawk habits, through bar stools and greenless parks,
beauty salons, floating games, going somewhere, haranguing the

crowds, his sleeves rolled up like a steel worker's, hurling epithets at the pharoah's club-wielding brigade, under orders to hunt down the first born of each low lit hearth.

There are no bulls in America in the sense of great symbols, which preside over resuscitation of godheads, that shake the dead land green. Only the "bull" of Birmingham, papier maché, ten dollars down monthly terms, carbon copy mock heroic American variety of bullhood, who told a crowded room of flashbulbs that there was an outsider moving in and out of things that night, a spectre who flashed through the night like pentecost.

He's right, there was.

Not the spook of the Judaic mystery, the universal immersed in the particular. Not the outsider from unpopular mysteries, a monstrous dialectic waddling through the corridors of his brain, but the nebulous presence hidden by flashbulbing events in Birmingham, Metempsychosis stroking the air.

Pragma the bitch has a knight errant called Abbadon, in the old texts the advocate of dreadful policies. The whore, her abominations spilling over, her stinking after-births sliming their way towards a bay of pigs, has a bland and well-groomed knight errant who said that "if we hand down a few more decisions, pile up paper, snap a few more pictures by Bachrach of famous people before grand rhetorical columns of the doric order, perhaps they will stop coming out into the streets in Raleigh, Greensboro, Jackson and Atlanta (sometimes called the Athens of the south).

Pragma's well-groomed and bland procurer is on long distance manufacturing heroes,
Heroes who bray in sirens screaming in from Idlewild, winging in from points south,
Their utterances cast into bronze by press-card-carrying harpies, those creatures of distorted reality.

O ebony-limbed Osiris, what clown folk singer or acrobat shall I place the tin wreath upon?
When will Osiris be scattered over 100 ghettoes?

110

Heroes are ferried in by motorcycle escorts, their faces cast into by
    Pointillism, by Artzybasheff,
Sculptor of Henry Luce's America.

Introducing the King of Birmingham, sometimes called the
    anointed one,
And receives the tin wreath across Americana banquet rooms,
His hands dripping with blood like a fanatical monk as rebellion
    squirms on the stake.

Introducing the Black Caligula, who performs a strip tease of the
    psyche,
Between Tiffany ads and Vat 69, giving up a little pussy for a
    well-groomed and bland knight errant.

O ebony-limbed Osiris, what knight club tap dancing charlatan
    shall I place the tin wreath upon?
All things are flowing said the poet when gods ambushed gods:
    Khan follows Confucius
    Light follows darkness
Tin wreathed heroes are followed by the figure in antique clothes,
    obscured by the flash-bulbing events in Birmingham.
Metempsychosis in the air.

NAOMI REPLANSKY

From *Ring Song*

... When that joy is gone for good
I move the arms beneath the blood.

When my blood is running wild
I sew the clothing of a child.

When that child is never born
I lean my breast against a thorn.

When the thorn brings me reprieve
I rise and live, I rise and live.

When I live from hand to hand
Nude in the marketplace I stand.

When I stand and am not sold
I build a fire against the cold.

When the cold comes creeping round
I seek a warmer stamping-ground.

When that ground becomes too small
I come against a stony wall.

When that wall is not to climb
I chalk on it a burning rhyme.

When the rhyme can work no spell
I know the circle of my hell.

When my hell does not destroy
I leap from ambush on my joy. . . .

TIM REYNOLDS

A Hell of a Day

This was a day of fumbling and petty accidents,
as though the population had grown all thumbs
at once. Watering her chrysanthemums,
Mrs. Kamei was surprised to see the plants
blacken, water turn to steam. Both Dote and Michiko
noted the other's absence but not her own.
Mr. Kime lifted his hat, but his head was gone.
Mr. Watanabe rolled a double zero.

Photographing her son by the river bridge
Mrs. Ume pressed the shutter and over exposed her film.
Her son's yawn swallowed him. And everything turned on
when pretty Miss Mihara snapped the light-switch.
Then old Mr. Ekahomo struck a match
to light his pipe, and the town caught, and dissolved in flame.

HARLAND RISTAU

Korea

where one meets the other
where the head would smother in pillowed
white nights of steel,
here in a vast tract
of blood unmeasured land
something is given birth
in protracted
shelvings of fire.

where one dies, the other, crawling
mist-bound, found against a banked up
shore of loneliness, lives bandaged
trench solitudes, sailing
raftward dreams of home,
mud-caked, listening
to window nights
shattered in lamps of saffron moments.

where one meets the other (East and West,
Brothers in Time, timelessly staring)
the sun washings streak horizons in scratches
of light; there, one, a khaki silence,
whose sentence rifle shall no longer
write flesh tunnel communication words,
leans in a corpse cry of wordless mouth, born in
sagging mists in the ebb of shadow-stoned humanity!

LUCY SMITH

No Man an Island

There is a part of me
That can never go home,
For I have known men who can never go home:
    the dice are thrown,
    the gamblers wait;
        I have known men who waited like this,
        who threw and lost—
        and now clutch nothing . . .

    the music blares,
    the dancers spin;
        I have known men who spun like this,
        at the impact of a bullet—
        they spin no more.

I sight along the cue,
I drop it unused;
        I have known men who sighted like this
        along the barrel of a gun—
        they sight no more.

There is part of me
That can never go home,
Part of me that will always lie still,
On some lonely beach head
    with the mines still unreaped
Where the waves of men flowed and ebbed like the tide.
Because I have known men who can never go home,
There is part of me
That can never go home.

RAY SMITH

On the Little Bighorn

(*For my father, W. R. Smith, a quartermaster sergeant in 1908 in South Dakota, where he grew up among stories of the Indian West. I served in the 4th Cavalry near the Black Hills in 1941.*)

1. THEN: The Sioux

That was our country, the Four Winds know it
From Bear Butte through the hills into Montana.
My people stayed out with Crazy Horse
When others untied the knots in their ponies' tails
And went in to the reservation as Three Star told them.

    This was the winter before Longhair's coming.
    The snow came, the first heavy snow,
    White everywhere, but the river dark and whirling.
    That was an empty time, the women glum,
    The Tepee hunger-silent, no cooking smell,
    But parched corn eaten under the buffalo robe . . .

We called our friends
From Lame Deer's tepee and Crow Passes'.
"Hoh-oh-oh. Come. We have buffalo. We have tobacco.
Come. Come. Feast and smoke with us."
There were many lodges with my people then.
Uncpapa, Blackfeet, Minneconjoux Sioux
In circles north from the Little Bighorn bend,
Arrows-All-Gone and Ogallala together,
And across a stream Cheyennes. Twelve thousand people.
Each lodge and each camp circle opened East.
Our chiefs were Sitting Bull of the Uncpapa,
Leading the old man chief of the encampment;

The Ogallalas' Crazy Horse, Lame Deer
of the Minneconjoux, Hump of Arrows-All-Gone,
Dirty Moccasin and Old Bear of the Cheyennes,
And Lame White Man the Cheyenne warrior chief.
Not many guns, and some were muzzle loading.
Some were lost in the Powder River burning.

GARY SNYDER

The Late Snow & Lumber Strike of the Summer of Fifty-Four

Whole towns shut down
    hitching the Coast road, only gypos
Running their beat trucks, no logs on
Gave me rides. Loggers all gone fishing
Chainsaws in a pool of cold oil
On back porches of ten thousand
Split-shake houses, quiet in summer rain.
Hitched north all of Washington
Crossing and re-crossing the passes
Blown like dust, no place to work.

Climbing the steep ride below Shuksan
    clumps of pine
      float out the fog
No place to think or work
    drifting.
On Mr. Baker, alone
In a gully of blazing snow:
Cities down the long valleys west
Thinking of work, but here,
Burning in sun-glare
Below a wet cliff, above a frozen lake,
The whole Northwest on strike
Black burners cold,

116

The green-chain still,
I must turn and go back:
      caught on a snowpeak
      between heaven and earth
And stand in lines in Seattle.
Looking for work.

YURI SUHL

The Permanent Delegate

My name is Jew.
   I come from the land of skeleton.
They beat me in Berlin,
      tortured me in Warsaw,
         shot me in Lublin
And I am still here—the ash of my bones
      a glowing monument, a fiery headstone.

I am the scorched hair of a virgin's bright curls
      smoothed and patted by anxious hands
I am a maddened mother's futile tears
      soothing in vain a hundred anguished hurts.

I am the spasm of a body convulsed in flames,
      the crumbling of a skeleton,
the boiling of blood, shriveling of flesh,
      smouldering ash of six million—
ashes of body, of brain, of vision, of work—
      ashes of genius and dreams,
         ashes of God's master stroke—Man

Count the limbs, gentlemen—
      match them if you can in pairs.
      It can't be done.
For I am one ghost of six million.

117

Out of all the ashes I have become one
And the dream lies broken and spit on.

I am here to tell you, gentlemen
    it's a lie—the world is not yet Hitler-free.
Millions see it, condemn it,
    cry out my pain and warn you.

But you are moved like a granite statue
    by the prick of a pin.
Therefore I have come,
    uninvited, unwelcome
        bringing a message
from the land of skeleton.

I am grafting my ash to your souls.
I am hanging my dreams around your necks.
I am blotting out the sun from your day
                with my shadow.
I am tearing the quiet of your night
                with the shrieks of my tortures.
I will beat at your conscience
    with the hands of a million dead children and
I will pick at your brains
                with my maggots.
Yea, though you split the atom to infinity
    you will see my face before your eyes.
I sit at all the round tables
At every conference I am a delegate,
my credentials signed by six million
    from the land of skeleton
and you will never get rid of me
    until the world is Hitler-free.

(translated from the Yiddish by Max Rosenfeld
and Walter Lowenfels)

ALAN SWALLOW

On the Outgoing Train

1. These little settlements
   Sediments of outrageous time
   Upon the dark north tundra—

   Echo the voice of trains
   Which chatter their iron wheels
   Over the worn face of the land.

   What have we left behind?
   Some harvest we meant to share
   In the sworn fiesta of home.

   Those sober houses, clustered
   But separate, sit quietly the plain
   Formal as the stone hand of love.

2. You fade down many tracks—
   On many roads I follow you.
   In Russia, China, Yugoslavia,
   Those foreign, yet familiar, faces
   Turn like kind and sober brothers
   To share our loneliness.

   Dear Love,
   Within their hope we find our home:
   We share their struggle and their fame;
   In all their lands you comfort them,
   In all their names they speak your name.

DALTON TRUMBO

From *For a Convict's Wife*

. . . Each man owes his country
    At least a little time in jail,
    So it cannot be a matter of surprise
    That I arrive at last before these gates
    Which have closed so many times on better men,
    And daily close upon my brothers . . .

There is something strange in this cell
The air in this place turns agitated.
The foundation walls carry distant tremors
And we are suddenly engulfed in sounds.

Do you feel them, my dear?
Do you hear this enormous tumult?
Did you hear that great shout from the throat of Asia?
Can you hear the howled obscenities of the last slaver
Riveting handcuffs and judicial decrees
That will never fit the clean black fist of Africa?
Do you hear the uneasy murmur of the Americas saying

                    Is this what you meant?
                    Were these the promises?
                    Can you build a jail that big?

Lift your clear eyes from this place, my dear:
Can you see them there,
Moving in light above the great horizon's arch,
All the lovely generations,
Bathed in the dew of morning,
Fresh with the touch of kisses,
Proud in brotherhood and sisterhood,

Free at last of all but each other,
And singing?
Can you see them, the people of earth, as they work? . . .

For a moment we were frightened
For an instant we stood alone.
For a time the darkness descended
And perhaps we were afraid.

But here in this warm and friendly light,
Among these hearty peoples of our own,
In this kaleidoscope of color and of tongues,
We stand together as always we have stood,
Your gentle hand in mine, and mine in yours.

And being now together while apart,
Never again shall we be separate.
And a year will make no difference,
And a thousand years will make no difference,
And never seeing each other again will make no difference,
And dying will make no difference.

For as friends and lovers and equals
We have sealed our treaty against the past:
We have drunk wild sacramental wine
And our children rise from the earth like flowers
Lifting their faces for tomorrow's sun.

PAUL VESEY

American Gothic

To Satch

*(The legendary Satchell Page, one of the star pitchers
in Negro baseball)*

Sometimes I feel like I will never stop
Just go on forever
Til one fine mornin'
I'm gonna reach up and grab me a handfulla stars
Swing out my long lean leg
And whip three hot strikes burnin' down the heavens
And look over at God and say
How about that!

MEL WEISBURD

Between Chicago and St. Paul

I had expected something quite different.
But this almost forgotten, familiar country
Sours with the headlines of the day's news:
The neutron bomb. Another incident . . .

Like a smooth war-machine, the torque
Of the earth turns the dark over
My clattering, yellow-streaked passage. From
The train, the peace is glaring and inconsolable.

The trees are gangrene with throttled sun.
The farms are galvanized for war.

The moon, melancholy, and out of mind,
Hurls a charge down the missile slopes.

But past the hostages, whose yellow lights
Cling like willows to the darkness,
And the metric of the neutral Mississippi
I return to make peace with my father,

To settle with my mother, mother of fact,
In whose counties the leaves drop with dispossession,
Who complains from the crippled distance to her Poland,
How all America stings in crabby rooms.

The Germans shot her in the head. I
Remember now that wound which never stood the heal,
Suppurating an unforgotten war. I suppose,
That tinny conflagration of 1914.

Because she is certified psychotic
I must make a compensation; I have learned,
Alone, to make my way in the unknown, to accept
How God chokes Minnesota into beauty.

Still, I configure my malaise on the window glass.
My breath stains the world as it passes.
In the dark, the human is a catastrophe,
The minute an unexploded moment.

It is not that I am afraid to die
With distance and escaping time,
But that we should all die at once,
Sends me slowly home.

NANCY WESTLAKE

Celle Qui Meurt

Crécy and Agadir, the siege at Acre,
the bridge at Poitiers, Novara, Saint-Mihiel;
the interminable wet war in Flanders;
the sluggish swarms of flies, the peacock cry
of someone spitted suddenly; the thrust
and plunge of rapine; laces torn
and silver cups and spiky crowns of gold
melted and puddled. In the marble snow,
stiffened in stubborn attitudes, the dead
resist interment in the frozen ground.

Death leaves the land
clean as a crow-picked bone: scoured
            with salt and fire.
Housewifely Death
complains because the work is never done
and muddy feet track in the blood again.

Nous avons changé tout cela.
Hiroshima.

JOSEPH WHITE

Black is a Soul

Down
Down into the fathomless depths
Down into the abyss beneath the stone
Down still farther, to the very bottom
    of the infinite
Where black-eyed peas & greens are stored

Where de lawd sits among melon rinds.
A dark blue sound (funky & barefooted)
        entered & sang a tear for the People
Of black women (buxom & beautiful)
With nappy heads & cocoa filled breasts
        nippled with molasses,
        & their legs sensual & long beneath
        short bright dresses
& of black men greasy from the sun-soaked
        fields sitting in the shade,
        their guitars, the willow & the
        squatting sun weeping authentic blues

These quantums of pure soul
Who pick cotton under the rant rays of the sun
Who eat hot greasy fish, chitlins, corn pone,
        pig feet, fat back & drink wine
        on Sat. nights
Who get happy & swing tambourines & sing
        them there spirituals
Who are blessed by the power of poverty
Who bathe their feet in streamlets of
        simplicity
Who are torn by the insolence & depression
        of bigot blonde America,
Are the essence of beauty
The very earth
The good earth
The black earth

In these moments when my man preaches
        about a no good nigger woman who did
        him wrong
My fingers begin to pop
My feet jump alive
The blue sound clutches me to its bosom
        until I become that sound
In these moments when the sun is blue

When the rivers flow with wine
When the neck bone tree is in blossom
I raise my down bent kinky head to charlie
    &shout
I'm black. I'm black
& I'm from Look Back

JONATHAN C. WILLIAMS

From *The Empire Finals at Verona*

in a twinkling
of a flash-boom
      ('pika-don')
of megatons:
        'it was at this moment
        that Hiroshima City,
        the culmination of many years' work,
        disappeared
        with its good citizens
        into the beautiful sky'

PS:
        'the peaches you brought us
        from Okayama
        the day before the pika-don
        were delicious'

O bored, au bord de la mer-
de, de la
reeking radiolog-
ical cali-
fornian seas,
incarnadined, baroqued incredibly
to the tongue

126

mute, flat on the planet,
eyeing a jet-stream eight miles out,
full of fall-out, waste and fragrance
from Nevada

going out to seed the plankton,
sink atolls
     and burst the livers of great whales

and Colorado ready to send green gas nervelessly,
coolly thru the quaking aspen, spewn
from its Denver arsenal

         (and me
         without my atropine styrette!)

only the gods got
       ichor in their bubbling veins,
                o Admiral
O !

SARAH E. WRIGHT

To Some Millions Who Survive Joseph Mander, Sr.

Sunday strollers along a sewage filled Schuykill
May soon forget where he died;
And many will point with second hand authority
To the place in liquid darkness
Showing only where
Death gave birth to a hero.
But they might glory in any novel bit
Of newsprint knowledge quite as pridefully,
Great men often become great curiosities;
Too often become conversation pieces, and nothing more.
But something should be said about Joseph E. Mander, Sr.

Lest the lesson he died to teach—follows him to death.
Joseph E. Mander, Sr., hero today and contemporary choice for
    parlor pledges
Is more than a name to you now.
Yesterday you didn't know him—didn't care to meet him.
To some of you (and I speak to that some of you)
He was any black man walking the streets of a segregated housing
    project;
Keeping in his "proper" place—staying close to his particular breed
    of dark skinned humanity.
Fenced in by stronger walls than stone and steel;
Forced in by will—your will—your fears—your hate.
Squeezed by your financial and legislative strength
into a specified "had to be enough" little plot of ground
To raise his three children and one more on the way,
Safely away from yours.
And after that yesterday, when you didn't know him,
Your favorite obligation now
Joseph Mander died.
Died proving what so many have tried
to obliterate with blood.
Remember Warsaw!
Remember blood?
Red, human life substance
Spilling all over your conscience,
Trying to wash away brotherhood!
            And yet it lives
Mander proved it—knew it—died because of it and you with your
    memories of blood.

Yes, one of your infant kind whose fear of the lone big silence,
Forced but one strangled plea for help;
Cared not a bit that it was a brown, fully clothed Mander,
Whose love directed body plunged into the river's filth,
Reaching out with his black hand—his life;
Even if it meant his own—and it did.
And it should be said that
Greater Fatherhood has no man than he

Who would leave those he had conceived
To return to life one
Whose "so called" superiority,
Might one day deny his flesh—his images—
Full and equal right to life.
Now I have seen monuments—great geometric heaps of stone;
Lifeless towers, raised to keep alive the dead.
And I have seen you, the people—anxious to write off
Your obligation to Mander and his survivors (there are 15 million
    of them)
With a hurried check—a few high-sounding speeches,
And if nothing spectacular happens
To claim the moments you've allowed for bigness,
You will remember the black man long enough
To raise a great grey stone thing—a feelingless symbol
In final payment.

But I ask—cannot a monument that breathes be built?
A grateful people are bigger than all the tall piled stones
In our wide and wondrous world.
A grateful people are wise when their living grows into a growing
    monument.
And I ask—will a monument breathe for Mander—spring out of
    the heart of the people who
Have grown wise in the ways of brotherhood as taught by brave
    dead Mander?
And I ask—
When you walk through the spring that won't come this year for
    Joseph Mander, Sr.
Will you turn those fingers that point to say "That's where our
    hero died"
Back to yourselves—point to your hearts saying "But this is where
    he lives?"

CARL YEARGENS

Shadows for the Sun
to G.N.P.

Another man has fled to Habana, Jorge,
a poet whose eyes were black suns,
in the lemon sky, his eyes were black suns.

He dreamt of home with rooms of love, Jorge,
having voyaged among dustbeds and stonewalks of exile,
tremolo of blue rivers, he sang with tongues of water . . .
a poet who wasted steel loaves in our heart,
wounds without suffering, and woke in an exile of wounds.
In Habana primeval libations drank his blood,
drumming nakedness, he remembered home and his tears.

Another man has come to Habana, Jorge,
a poet whose words are red suns,
upon the black earth, his words are red suns.

With furrow plowed and brick lain, Jorge,
opening the deepwells of mountains and humble arms
against the honeyed mouth in the rotting head
that buried in bee's whir sucks a dead flower,
has stung its last dream, a poet whose passion
is a child's reaching hand, a man's machete
hunger, an island's only hope, the island of Man.

And you, another to flee to Habana, Jorge,
a poet whose words are green sails,
over red crests, your eyes are black sails.
O tell me, how shall we dream and create, Jorge,
Even simple pigeons flee the siren's iron.
We can't. Our home is our exile, our flesh
our crime; and if we were to hate and found
mountains for our hate, will we be able to thwart

the taste of ivory? Sinking in the currents
of coin, chased to death, we'll write shadows for the sun.

Other men will come to Habana, Jorge,
other men whose hearts would read the sea,
almost dying of hate, they will come to read the sea.

CURTIS ZAHN

Antiwarwoman

She made the skies with eyes like
Two or three wounded doves
And in a delicate mourn for peace
      Forgave them their wars
While the Generals, late for their Martinis & Olives
And, I suppose, destiny
Clicked shut their minds, their brief
      Cases, and called
      For Cadillacs;
Their famed, buttonpushing fingers
Concealed at all times
From the wistful soil of public gaze
By immaculate gloves.
      And she counted the stars
Lately to be subdivided by Nucleotheorists
With their perplexed mathematics of some
      Simply smashing plan
For the abolition of hunger, poverty, and world itself
While nibbling an O'Henry bar
Meant for some oriental child.
And now also unsure of her warmth & clothing
In that muscular affluence of cost-plus unity
She put her placard aside
And went into the restroom where unsegregated women
Sat alongside
The bewildered constituents of Democracy.

131

Biographical Notes

GEORGE ABBE: Born 1911 in New England; has lived there most of his life. He is editor of the Book Club for Poetry. In addition to five novels and a play, his books include the following volumes of poetry: *Wait For These Things* (N.Y., Henry Holt, 1940); *Letter Home* (1944); *The Wide Plains Roar* (Conway, N.H., World Fellowship, 1954); *Bird in the Mulberry* (1954); *The Incandescent Beast* (1957). His poem "Changed" appears in *Collected Poems* (Peterboro, N.H., Richard R. Smith, 1961).

GEORGE BASS: Born 1939, Nashville, Tennessee; secretary and literary assistant to Langston Hughes. His television shows have been produced over WNBC in New York. His poem "Life Cycle in the Delta" is in manuscript.

JOHN BEECHER: Born in Birmingham, Alabama, 1905; has published a number of volumes of poetry, including *Report to the Stockholders*, Selected Poems (Phoenix, Arizona, Rampart Press, 1962), re-issued in paper back (N.Y., Monthly Review Associates, 1963); *In Egypt Land* (Phoenix, 1960); *Phantom City* (Phoenix, 1961). "A Veteran's Day of Recollection" appeared in the magazine *Brand X*.

ART BERGER: A New York printer, born in New York, 1920. His book *Blow the Man Down* was published by *Poetry* (London/New York, 1962). "Bedford Avenue" appeared in *Umbra*.

ALVAH BESSIE: Born 1904, New York city; now lives in San Francisco. He has written five novels, many short stories and an autobiography. A member of the Abraham Lincoln Brigade, he edited the anthology *Heart of Spain*. From 1943–1950 he wrote for the screen; was jailed in 1950 for "contempt of congress" as one of the Hollywood Ten. "For My Dead Brother" is from *Masses & Mainstream* (July 1953).

MILLEN BRAND: Born 1906, Jersey City. He has two books of poems nearing completion; his poems have appeared in many magazines. He has written four novels and many short stories and, with Frank Partos, wrote the script of the motion picture *The Snake Pit*. "Local Light" is from the magazine *Chicago Choice*, 1961.

132

GEORGE BRATT: Born 1893, Michigan; carpenter and active trade union-
ist; educated here and abroad; worked in avant-garde theatre in 1920's; is
also a photographer. "A.W.O.L." appears in *On the Bosses' Time* (San
Francisco, Bay Ridge Publishers, 1958). New book in preparation.

MARION BUCHMAN: Born in Baltimore, she has written poetry since
early childhood. Her work has appeared in numerous publications. "First-
born" is from *Voice in Raman* (New York, Bookman Associates, 1959).

CHARLES BUKOWSKI: Born in Germany, 1920; came to the U.S. at two.
Widely published in magazines, his books include: *It Catches My Heart in
Its Hands: Selected Poems 1955–1963* (Loujon Press); *Flower, Fist and
Bestial Wall* (Hearse Press); *Run With the Hunted* (Midwest Poetry
Chapbook). "The Day I Kicked a Bankroll Out the Window" comes from
Longshot Poems for Broke Players (New York, 7 Poets Press, 1962).

OLGA CABRAL: Born in the West Indies; now lives in Long Beach, N.Y.
Her first volume was *Cities and Deserts* (N.Y., Roving Eye Press, 1959),
from which "Empire State" was selected.

ALVARO CARDONA-HINE: Born 1928 in Costa Rica, he now lives in
Hollywood. He is one of the editors of the magazine *Coastlines*. His book
of Haiku poems was published in 1962 (Alan Swallow, Denver). "Bulosan
Now" is from *Mainstream*, 1956.

JOHN WILLIAM CORRINGTON: Born 1932 in Shreveport, Louisiana,
his first volume of poems was published in 1962 by Charioteer Press. A
novel, *And Wait For the Night*, was published 1964. *Mr. Clean and Other
Poems* is in preparation for publication by the San Francisco Review. His
work has appeared in numerous publications. "Communique: I" appeared in
The Anatomy of Love, Roman Books, Ft. Lauderdale, Fla., 1964.

GREGORY CORSO: Born New York City, 1932. His books include: *The
Vestal Lady on Brattle* (Cambridge, 1955); *Happy Birthday of Death* (New
York, New Directions, 1962); *Long Live Man* (Norfolk, Conn., New Di-
rections, 1962). "Uccello" comes from *Gasoline* (San Francisco, City
Lights, 1958).

CARLO CORTEZ: Born in 1923, Milwaukee. An active pacifist and con-
tributor to the *Industrial Worker*, in which "Outa Work Blues" first appeared. His work has also been published in *Beatitude East*.

MARGARET DANNER: Born in Kentucky. In 1952, *Poetry*, Chicago (of
which she later became assistant editor), published a series of her poems,

"Far From Africa." She lives in Detroit and has received a number of awards and honors, the most recent being the John Hay Whitney Award. Her work appears in *Beyond the Blues, New Poems by American Negroes*, edited by Rosy Pool (Lympne, Kent, England, Hand and Flower Press, 1962). "The Elevator Man Adheres to Form" is in manuscript.

RICHARD DAVIDSON: Born 1929 in Chicago. He has published poems in many magazines, and his short dramatic pieces have been produced in Greenwich Village coffee houses. "Play the Last March Slowly" is from the magazine *Liberation*, 1959.

WALT DELEGALL: Born 1936, Philadelphia. He is a student at Howard and editor of *Dasein*, a "national quarterly of the arts," started in 1960 by the Howard Poets. "Elegy for a Lady" is from *Beyond The Blues*.

RAY DUREM: Born 1915, Seattle, died in 1963. A veteran of the Spanish Civil War, he has lived in many parts of the United States and Mexico. He has published in a number of magazines, and a collection of his poetry is in preparation. "Award" is in manuscrpt.

BOB DYLAN: Born in Minnesota, 1941, known primarily as an outstanding composer and lyricist in the contemporary folk song revival. He has made recordings for Columbia and Folkway Records. "Hard Rain's Gonna Fall" appears here for the first time as a poem; the lyric is reprinted from *Sing Out*, the New York folk song magazine.

EILEEN EGAN: A native of Wales, living in New York. Her work has appeared in *Integrity, Sign* and other magazines (sometimes under the pen name J. O'Sullivan-Barra). Her poem "Hibakusha" appeared in the magazine *Peace*. She is preparing two books for publication.

MARI EVANS: Born in Toledo, Ohio. Now writing and educating her two sons in Indianapolis. She has been a civil service employee, song writer and choir director. Her poem "Status Symbol" is in manuscript.

LAWRENCE FERLINGHETTI: Born 1919, New York; reached San Francisco 1951; built a bookstore; began to publish the *Pocket Book Series*, which includes the work of Allen Ginsberg, Gregory Corso and Kenneth Patchen. *Starting from San Francisco* was published by New Directions, New York, 1962, and includes the poem "Tentative Description of a Dinner for the Impeachment of Eisenhower." Other books include *A Coney Island of the Mind; Her*, a novel; and *Unfair Arguments with Existence*, also published by New Directions.

VINCENT FERRINI: Born 1913, Saugus, Mass. Has worked as teacher, bench hand, shoe worker; now makes picture frames in Gloucester, Mass. His poetry has appeared in Japan, Mexico, France, Australia, Canada, England. Among his published works: *Five Plays* (London, The Fortune Press, 1959); *The Plow in the Ruins* (Prairie City, Ill., James A. Decker, 1946); *Book of One* (London, Villers, 1960); *Injunction* (Lynn, Mass., Sand Piper Publishers, 1943); *The House of Time* (London, Fortune, 1953). "The Sea" is from *Mirandum*, Heuretic Press, 1953.

EDWARD FIELD: Born 1924, Brooklyn. He has published poems in many magazines; "Ode to Fidel Castro" is from his book, *Stand Up Friend, With Me* (N.Y., Grove Press, 1963), which won the Lamont Poetry Award.

GENE FRUMKIN: Born 1928, New York City; now lives in Los Angeles. His poems have appeared in a number of magazines. *The Hawk and the Lizard*, a volume of poetry, is in preparation for publication by Alan Swallow. He also has two novels in preparation, and was one of the editors of *Coastlines*. "In the Margin of the Text" is in manuscript.

DAVID GALLATIN: Born 1926, Miami, Florida. He was brought up on a farm in Tennessee and now lives in New York. Author of *Machines and Illusions*. He has several books in preparation for publication. "Put Your Key" appears in *Love and Its Loves* (New York, 1962).

ESTELLE GERSHGOREN: Born 1940, Detroit. She lives in Los Angeles, where she graduated from the University of California. "We Are Gathered Together" is in manuscript.

JACK GILBERT: A young West Coast poet whose work has appeared in a number of magazines. "The Abnormal is Not Courage" is from *Jeopardy* (New Haven, Yale University Press, 1962).

ALLEN GINSBERG: Born 1926, Paterson, N.J. Has published in many magazines. His books include: *Howl* (San Francisco, City Lights, 1960); *Empty Mirrors* (Totem Corinth, New York, 1961); *Reality Sandwiches* (City Lights, 1963). "Kaddish" appears in his volume *Kaddish* (City Lights, 1961).

DON GORDON: Born in Connecticut, now lives in Los Angeles and has been published widely in many magazines. Among his books are: *Statement* (1946), and *Displaced Persons* (Denver, Alan Swallow, 1958), from which his poem "The Kimono" is quoted.

135

ROBERT HAYDEN: Born 1913, Detroit. His published work includes *Heartshape in the Dust* (1940) and *Ballad of Remembrance* (London, Paul Bremen, 1962), in which "Middle Passage" appears. In that book the author notes "this poem follows the account of the Amistad Mutiny related by Muriel Rukeyser in her biography of Willard Gibbs."

LESLIE WOOLF HEDLEY: Born in New Jersey; now lives in San Francisco. His work is widely printed in magazines. His books, published by Inferno Press, San Francisco, include: *The Edge of Insanity* (1949); *Death of a World* (1951); *Selected Poems* (1953); *Abraxas and Other Poems* (1960). His *Collected Poems* is in preparation. "Chant for all the People on Earth" appeared in the magazine *Miscellaneous Man* (San Francisco).

BARBARA HINCHCLIFFE: A Philadelphia poet, born 1923, whose work has appeared in Quaker magazines and in *Liberation*. "A Sunday in the Thirties" is from manuscript.

CARL WENDELL HINES, JR.: Born 1940, North Carolina. His poetry has appeared in various magazines and also in the collection *American Negro Poetry* (N.Y., 1963). "Jazz Poem" is in manuscript.

GEORGE HITCHCOCK: Born 1914, Hood River, Oregon. He is the author of seven plays, and many of his short stories have appeared in anthologies. His poems have been published in a number of magazines and in his book *Poems and Rivers* (San Francisco, 1962). "The Indestructible" appeared in *Mainstream*.

FRANK HORNE: Born 1899, New York. Known in the 20's for his poems *Letters Found Near a Suicide*, which won a *Crisis* award, he recently resumed writing, after a shattering illness, with a new cycle of poems, *Haverstraw* (London, Paul Bremen, 1963). "Resurrection" is in manuscript.

HERSCHEL HORN: Born in Detroit, he was brought up on the West Coast and now lives in New York, where he teaches school. Has published a number of poems in magazines. His poem "Landscape Near a Steel Mill" appeared in *Mainstream* (May 1957) under the *nom de plume*, John Frazer.

LANGSTON HUGHES: Born 1902, Joplin, Missouri. His published volumes include: *The Negro Speaks of Rivers; Crisis 1921–1925; Weary Blues* (1926); *The Langston Hughes Reader* (1958); *Selected Poems* (New York, Knopf, 1958). "Let America be America Again" is a 1964 revision of a poem that was originally published in part in *Esquire* (July 1936) and appeared in *The Poetry of the Negro* (New York, 1949).

CHARLES HUMBOLDT: Born in 1910, died in 1964. He was managing editor of Art Front in the 30's; after the war served on the staff of New Masses, as an editor of Mainstream till 1960, and later on the editorial staff of The National Guardian. His poems and stories have appeared in various magazines. A volume of his collected writings is in preparation. "Field of Plunder" is from Mainstream.

JOE JOHNSON: Born in New York, 1940. Has written a documentary film on the South, "Black and Blue." His poems have appeared in Umbra. "Judeebug's Country" is in manuscript.

KAY JOHNSON: A young New Orleans painter and poet, who now lives in Greece. Her poems have appeared in The Outsider, Olympia and other magazines. A volume of her poems, Human Songs, has been published (San Francisco, City Lights, 1964). "A Defiant Song" is from a manuscript collection.

LEROI JONES: Born 1934, Newark, New Jersey. He has published in many magazines; is an editor of Yugen (Totem Press) and an associate editor of Kulchur. He edited The Moderns (New York, Corinth, 1963). His Preface to a Twenty-Volume Suicide Note was published in 1960 (New York, Totem). He also wrote Blues People (New York, Morrow, 1963) and a forthcoming book of fiction, The System of Dante's Hell (New York, Grove Press). "A Contract" is included in The Dead Lecturer (New York, Grove Press, 1964).

AARON KURTZ: Born 1891, Osve, Russia, died 1964. Lived in New York since childhood, and has published seven volumes of poetry in Yiddish: Chaos, 1920; Figaro, 1924; Placards, 1927; The Golden City, 1935; No Pasaran, 1938; Moishe Olgin, 1940; Marc Chagall, 1947. He has edited a number of magazines, including Heintike Lieder (Poems of Today). "Behold the Sea" appeared in Jewish Currents, January 1957.

PETER LA FARGE: Born in 1931, in Colorado. Known as a leading folksinger and composer. Part Indian, he specializes in songs of the Indian people. "Vision of a Past Warrior" is a song and appears here for the first time as a poem. It is part of his record "As Long as the Grass Shall Grow" (Folkways, New York, 1963).

CARL LARSEN: Born 1935, Hermosa Beach, California. Has had 250 poems and stories published in various magazines. A novel, The Book of Eric Hammerscoffer, is in preparation at Poet's Press, Washington, D.C. His first book is The Plot to Assassinate the Chase National Bank (New York, 7 Poet's Press, 1961), and the poem of the same name appears in that volume.

DENISE LEVERTOV: Born 1923, England, now lives in New York. Widely published in magazines, her books include: *The Double Image* (London, Cresset, 1946); *Here and Now* (San Francisco, City Lights, 1957); *Overland to the Islands* (Highlands, N.C., Jargon, 1958); *With Eyes at the Back of Our Heads* (New York, New Directions, 1959); *O Taste and See* (New York, New Directions, 1964). "Matins" is from *The Jacob's Ladder* (New York, New Directions, 1961).

JACK LINDEMAN: Born 1924, Philadelphia, has published poems in *Harper's Bazaar, Poetry, New World Writing*, and many other newspapers and magazines. He is editor and publisher of the magazine, *Whetstone*. His *Twenty-One Poems* was published in 1963 by Atlantis Editions, Pampolona. "Lament for the Frontiers of the Empire" appeared in *The Minority Of One*.

WALTER LOWENFELS: Born 1897, New York City. Early books published in France and England (1929–34) were followed by career as journalist in Philadelphia. He resumed publication of poetry in 1955. Edited *Walt Whitman's Civil War* (New York, Knopf, 1960). Volumes published include: *The Suicide* (Paris, Carrefour, 1934); *Sonnets of Love and Liberty* (New York, Blue Heron Press, 1955); *American Voices* (New York, Roving Eye Press, 1959); *Imaginary Daughter* (Horizon Press, New York, 1964). "Letter to the President" appeared in *Renaissance* and in *Political Affairs*.

RICHARD LYONS: Born 1920, in Detroit; lives in North Dakota. His poetry has appeared in various magazines and several volumes of his work are in preparation. "Goodbye the Office" appeared in *Men and Teakettles* (Denver, Alan Swallow, 1956).

WILLIAM J. MARGOLIS: Born Pittsburgh Pennsylvania, 1927; has published in many magazines including *Beatitude, Beloit Poetry Journal, Colorado Review; East and West* (India); *The Miscellaneous Man* (which he edited), *San Francisco Review* and *Trace*. His books are: *The Anteroom of Hell*, (San Francisco, Inferno Press, 1957); *The Little Love of Our Yearning* (San Francisco, Miller/McNail, 1962).

JAMES BOYER MAY: Born 1904 in Wisconsin; now lives in Los Angeles, where he edits the magazine *Trace* (also published in London). Author of a number of books of criticism and essays and a leading authority in the little magazine field through *Trace* (which serves also as a guide in this field). His *Selected Poems, 1950–55* was published in 1955 (San Francisco, Inferno). The poem "Reflection After Empire" comes from the last-named volume.

STUART McCARREL: Born 1923, Chicago, an electrical engineer whose poems have appeared in *Choice, Brand X, Catalyst.* His "The Assassinations 1963" is from a manuscript book of poems.

MICHAEL McCLURE: San Francisco poet, born 1932. His work has appeared in many magazines, and he is the author of: *Hymns To St. Geryon & Other Poems* (San Francisco, Auerhan Press, 1959); *The New Book* (New York, Grove Press, 1961); *Dark Brown* (Auerhan Press, 1961); *Meat Science Essays* (City Lights, 1964). "Fidelio" appeared in the magazine *Pa'Lante.*

THOMAS McGRATH: Born 1918, on a North Dakota Farm. His published work includes: *Dialectics of Love,* which appeared in *Three Young Poets* (Denver, Swallow, 1942); *To Walk A Crooked Mile* (New York, Swallow Press and Wm. Morrow, 1947); *Long Shot O'Leary's Garland of Practical Poesy* (New York, International, 1949); *Figures from a Double World* (Swallow, 1955); and *Letters to an Imaginary Friend* (Denver, Swallow, 1962)—from which the poem in this anthology is a fragment.

EVE MERRIAM: Born 1916, Philadelphia. Her *Family Circle* won the Yale Series of Younger Poets Prize in 1946. She has written many volumes of prose and poetry, among them: *Tomorrow Morning* (New York, Twayne, 1953); *Montgomery Alabama, Money, Mississippi and Other Places* (New York, Cameron Associates, 1956); *The Double Bed* (Cameron Associates, 1958). She has written a number of books of verse for children and a biography of Emma Lazarus. "Block Party" is from *Tomorrow Morning.*

MAY MILLER: Born in Washington, D.C. Has collaborated in two collections of plays about Negro life and history. Her volume *Into the Clearing* was published in 1959 (Washington, D.C., Charioteer Press), and she has had a number of poems in literary magazines. "The Last Warehouse" appeared in the anthology *Beyond the Blues.*

J. M. MURPHY: Born 1932, Washington, D.C. Was managing editor of first issue of *Chicago Choice* (March 1961); reads poetry on radio stations in Chicago and night clubs in New York. His poems have appeared in *Chicago Choice, Poetry Dial, The Critic, Dublin Review, Odyssey.* "The Flagmakers" appeared in the magazine *Rong Wrong.*

HOWARD McCORD: In his 30's, lives and teaches in the state of Washington. Author of "Precise Fragments," Dublin, 1963 and a book in manuscript "Bone," from which "Two There Are I Wish to Celebrate" is taken.

139

MYRON O'HIGGINS: Born in Chicago, 1918. He has published poems in magazines, in anthologies, including *American Negro Poetry* (edited by Arna Bontemps); and in *The Lion and the Archer*, published jointly with Robert Hayden, 1948. "Sunset Horn" comes from *American Negro Poetry*.

JOEL OPPENHEIMER: Born 1930, Yonkers, New York, now lives in New York City. Published volumes include: *The Dutiful Son* (Highlands, N.C., Jargon, 1957); *The Love Bit* (New York, Totem, 1960). His poem "17–18 April, 1961" appeared in the magazine *The Floating Bear* (1961).

RAYMOND PATTERSON: Born 1929, New York. Author of short stories and a novel. His poems have appeared in *Sixes and Sevens* (London, 1962), *Beyond the Blues*, and *Umbra*. "In Time of Crisis" is in manuscript.

IRENE PAULL: Born in Duluth, she now lives in San Francisco. She helped to organize the first CIO newspaper (*Midwest Labor*, Duluth) and wrote for it for many years. Her book of poems and sketches, *We're the People*, was published by *Midwest Labor*, 1942. Her poem "To Bill Heikkila, American" appeared in the San Francisco *People's World*; her poems and prose pieces have appeared in *Mainstream*, *Jewish Currents* and elsewhere.

ANNE PETERS: Born in Ireland, married an American and now lives in Connecticut. She has been published in various magazines and newspapers. "Kevin O'Culihain, Zorro Tio of the Andes, Exile" is in manuscript.

WILLIAM PILLIN: Born in the Ukraine, he now lives in California. *Dance Without Shoes* was a selection of the Book Club for Poetry and won the Jeanette Sewell Davis Prize in 1937. His first book, *Poems*, was published in 1939 (James Decker). "Miserere" is from *Passage After Midnight* (San Francisco, Inferno Press Editions, 1951.)

ALAN PLANZ: Born 1937, in New York. He has been published in a number of magazines, including *Poetry*, *Massachusetts Review*, *The Nation* and *Yugen*. He is co-editor of a new anthology of poems on civil rights. "Conjecture for a Short Mechanic" is in manuscript.

WILLIAM J. POMEROY: Born in Rochester, N.Y., 1915. Writer of short stories, history, articles. His only published poems are a group of 74 sonnets, *Seed*, (Chapel Hill, Transient Press, December 1962), from which "Beyond Barriers" is taken. The sonnets were written to his wife, a Filipina, while they were both serving ten years in jail for activities in the Philippine independence movement. *The Forest* (New York, International Publishers, 1963) is a personal account of his two years with the Huk guerrilla forces.

ISHMAEL REED: Born Tennessee, 1938. Now living in New York, he has published in *Mainstream, Liberator,* and *Umbra.* He has worked as a correspondent for the *Empire Star Weekly* in Buffalo. "The Ghost of Birmingham" appeared in *Liberator.*

NAOMI REPLANSKY: Grew up in New York City; lived for a period in France; now lives in California. Has written verse since she was ten and has been widely published. She is a translator of French and German poetry. "Ring Song" is from her volume of the same name (New York, Charles Scribner's Sons, 1952).

TIM REYNOLDS: Born Vicksburg, Mississippi, 1937; has published in various magazines including *The Nation, Saturday Review, Poetry, Atlantic.* His book *Ryoanki,* was published by Harcourt Brace, New York, 1964. "A Hell of a Day" is in manuscript.

HARLAND RISTAU: Born 1927, Milwaukee. His verse has appeared in 50 or more magazines. His books include *Slum School* (privately printed, 1953); *Next Time You're Alive* (New York, 7 Poets Press, 1962). "Korea" originally appeared in the magazine *Neon,* Brooklyn, N.Y.

LUCY SMITH: Born in Wilmington, North Carolina; now lives in Philadelphia. Her work has appeared in *Crisis* and other magazines. *No Middle Ground* was published in 1951 (Philadelphia). She was the co-author of *Give Me a Child* (Philadelphia, 1955).

RAY SMITH: Born 1915, Indianapolis; now lives in Iowa. Won Bridgeman Poetry Award for three successive years; edited a literary quarterly. His work has appeared in *Poetry* and other magazines. His *No Eclipse* was published in 1945 (Prometheus Press). "On the Little Bighorn" is from an unpublished manuscript.

GARY SNYDER: Born 1930, San Francisco; raised on farm near Seattle. His *Myths & Texts* was published in 1960 (New York, Totem/Corinth, 1960). "The Late Snow & Lumber Strike of the Summer of Fifty-Four" appeared in *Riprap* (Ashland, Mass., Origin, 1959).

YURI SUHL: Born 1908, in Poland; came to U.S. in 1923. He has published four volumes of poetry in Yiddish and two novels in English: *One Foot in America* (1950) and *Cowboy on a Wooden Horse* (1953), both published by Macmillan, New York. He also published *Ernestine Rose and The Battle for Human Rights* (New York, Reynal, 1959). "Permanent Delegate" is a revised version of a translation which appeared in *Opinion.*

ALAN SWALLOW: Born 1915, in Wyoming. Now lives in Denver. He is the founder of the publishing firm which bears his name. A former teacher, he is author of several volumes of poetry and has edited several magazines. His works include: *The War Poems of Alan Swallow* (1948); *Nameless Site: Poems 1937–57* (Prairie Press, 1956). "On the Outgoing Train" is quoted from the last-named volume.

DALTON TRUMBO: Known mainly as a playwright, was born in Colorado, 1905, co-founding editor of *The Screen Writer;* author of several novels, including *Johnny Got His Gun;* and many motion pictures, among them: *The Brave One* (Academy Award 1957), *Spartacus,* and *Exodus.* "For a Convict's Wife" appeared in *Mainstream,* July 1959.

PAUL VESEY: Born 1917, Samuel Allen is the name he uses as teacher and practitioner of law. His poetry has appeared recently in *Présence Africaine* and in *Beyond the Blues,* where "American Gothic" appeared. A volume of his poetry, *Ivory Tusks,* has been published in Germany.

MEL WEISBURD: Born in 1927, in St. Paul, he is now a resident of Los Angeles. He was formerly an editor of *Coastlines,* Los Angeles, and has been published in numerous magazines. "Between Chicago and St. Paul" appeared in the Chicago magazine *Midwest.*

NANCY WESTLAKE: A young West Coast poet. Her poem "Celle Qui Meurt" appeared in the Pacific Coast Magazine *Contact* (August 1962).

JOSEPH WHITE: Born in Philadelphia; now lives in Montauk Point, N.Y. His poems have appeared in the magazine *Dasein.* His "Black is a Soul" was published in the magazine *Burning Spear,* 1963, an anthology of Afro-Saxon poetry (Washington, D.C., Jupiter Hammon Press).

JONATHAN C. WILLIAMS: Born 1929, Asheville, North Carolina. He publishes the *Jargon* books of poetry. His own books include: *Red/Gray* (1952); *Four Stoppages* (1953); *Amen Huzza Selah* (Black Mountain, Jargon Press, 1956–59); *In England's Green &* (San Francisco, Auerhahn Press, 1962). "Empire Finals at Verona" comes from his volume of the same name (Highlands, N.C., Jargon, 1959).

SARAH E. WRIGHT: Born on the Eastern shore of Maryland. Her poems have appeared in several anthologies. She is the co-author of *Give Me A Child* (Philadelphia, 1951). Her first novel is scheduled for publication. "To Some Millions Who Survive Joseph Mander, Sr.," appeared in *Give Me A Child.*

CARL YEARGENS: Born 1937, in New York City, where he graduated from City College. He lives and works in New York. This poem "Shadows for the Sun" is in manuscript.

CURTIS ZAHN: Born in Detroit, Michigan, "over 40, under 60." Writer of poetry, essays, articles widely published in magazines. Thirteen of his poems appear in the magazine *Crazy Horse, 2*. A collection of his short stories *American Contemporary* was published by New Directions, New York, 1963.